MODI@11

Team Modi's
Eleven Year journey towards
Viksit Bharat

MODI@11

Team Modi's
Eleven Year journey towards
Viksit Bharat

Editor

AMIT GARG

GYAN

Published by

Gyan Publishing House
5, Ansari Road
Daryaganj, New Delhi-110002
Phone: 011-47034999, 9811692060
E-mail: books@gyanbooks.com

Distribution Network
gyanbooks.com
India, USA, Canada, UK, Australia, France

ISBN: 978-93-7414-803-7 (HB)

First Published, 2025

Printed at: Gyan Press, Delhi.

MODI@11:
Team Modi's Eleven Year journey towards Viksit Bharat
Edited by: AMIT GARG

Contents

List of Contributors

Prof. Abhijit Dutta, VC, Sikkim University.

Dr. Amit Ganatra, Provost (VC), Parul University

Prof. (Dr.) Ankur Kulkarni, VC, SAGE University

Prof. Anusha C Koti, Assistant Prof. of Law at KLE Law College

Bhavana Devi Tekcham, Research Scholar, Ancient History, and Archaeology Department, Manipur University

Prof. (Dr.) Debashis Bandyopadhyay, VC, KISS-DU, Bhubaneswar

Prof. Dhanawantri L. Singha, Assistant Prof., RNTU, Hojai, Assam

Dr. Hidam Ajit Meetei, Assi. Prof., Manipur University

Dr. J. M. Vyas, VC, National Forensic Sciences University, Gujarat

Prof. Javed Musarrat, VC, Integral University, Lucknow

Dr. Jayanthi V, VC, Sapthagiri NPS University, Bengaluru

Prof. K. K. Aggarwal, President, South Asian University

Prof. (Dr.) K P Yadav, VC, Mats University, Raipur, Chhattisgarh

Prof. Dr. K. Prathapan, VC, D. Y. P A & T University, Maharashtra

Dr. K Satyanarayan Reddy, VC, Srinivas University, Mangalore, Karnataka

Hon'ble Lt. General K. T. Parnaik, Governor of Arunachal Pradesh

Lt. Gen. (Dr.) Konsam Himalay Singh, Lt. Gen. (Ret.) of the Indian Army

Er. Kordor Lamare, Executive Engineer (WR), Dept. of Water Resources

Dr. Krishnan Chalil, Head, Central University of South Bihar, Gaya

Prof. (Dr.) Madan Mohan Goel, VC, Starex University, Gurugram

Prof. Manabendra Dutta Choudhury, VC, RNTU, Hojai, Assam

Prof. (Dr.) Manpreet Singh Manna, VC, Chandigarh University, Punjab

Dr. Mohammad Samir Hussain, Post Doctoral Fellow, Manipur University

Dr. N Vani Shree, Principal, JSS Law College, Mysuru, Karnataka

Dr. Nagaraj Ramrao, VC, Mohan Babu University, Andhra Pradesh

Prof. (Dr.) Narasingha Charan Panda, VC, Central University of Odisha

Dr. Naresh Kumar Tiwari, VC SAM Global University, Madhya Pradesh

Dr. Priyesh P. Gandhi, VC, Sigma University, Vadodara

Dr. Radha Krishan Dhiman, Director, SGPGIMS., Lucknow

Prof. (Dr.) Raj Kumar Kothari, VC, The Sanskrit College & University, Kolkata

Prof. (Dr.) Rajeev Bhardwaj, Pro VC, DBS Global University, Dehradun

Dr. Rajeev Manhas and Pratibha, Deputy Librarian & Head, Baba Farid University of Health Sciences, Punjab

Ms. Rajeswari H, Principal, JSS Law College, Mysuru, Karnataka

Prof. (Dr.) Rajul K. Gajjar, VC, Gujarat Technological University

Prof. Santosh Kumar Tripathy, VC, Fakir Mohan University, Balasore, Odisha

Dr. Shyam Sundar Rath, VC, National Sports University, Manipur

Prof. Som Nath Sachdeva, VC, Kurukshetra University, Kurukshetra

Dr. Sudhir Kumar Sharma, Director, Placement Cell, SGSU, Gujarat

Prof. (Dr.) Surender Kashyap, VC, Atal Medical & Research University, HP

Dr. Tankeshwar Kumar, VC, Central University of Haryana, Mahendergarh

Vijnana Bharti, Madhya Bharat Prant, SAM Global University

Acharya Devvrat
Governor, Gujarat
Gandhinagar-382021

आचार्य देवव्रत
राज्यपाल, गुजरात
गांधीनगर - ३८२०२१

संदेश

भारत ने पिछले ग्यारह वर्षों में जिन अभूतपूर्व क्षेत्रों में प्रगति की है, वह केवल संख्यात्मक विकास नहीं, बल्कि विचारधारा, दृष्टिकोण और नीतिगत क्रियान्वयन का भी प्रमाण है। प्रधानमंत्री श्री नरेन्द्रभाई मोदीजी के नेतृत्व में भारत सरकार ने 'सबका साथ, सबका विकास, सबका विश्वास और सबका प्रयास' के मूलमंत्र के साथ राष्ट्र के सर्वांगीण उत्थान का संकल्प लिया और उसे धरातल पर सफलतापूर्वक लागू किया।

इस कालखण्ड में अनेक ऐतिहासिक निर्णय हुए, जैसे कि स्वच्छ भारत मिशन, उज्ज्वला योजना, जन-धन योजना, डिजिटल इंडिया, आत्मनिर्भर भारत अभियान, नई शिक्षा नीति, प्राकृतिक कृषि को बढ़ावा और वैश्विक स्तर पर भारत की प्रतिष्ठा में निरंतर वृद्धि। यह सभी पहलें भारत की सांस्कृतिक जड़ों से जुड़ी हुई होने के साथ-साथ आधुनिक भारत की आकांक्षाओं को भी पूरा करती हैं।

प्रधानमंत्री श्री मोदीजी के नेतृत्व में शासन की कार्यसंस्कृति में पारदर्शिता, उत्तरदायित्व और कार्य-कुशलता का नवविस्तार हुआ है। साथ ही, भारत की आत्मा - ग्राम, किसान और युवाओं को केंद्र में रखकर बनाई गई नीतियों ने एक 'नए भारत' की नींव रखी है।

मैं इस बात से आश्वस्त हूं कि ज्ञान बुक्स प्रा. लि. द्वारा प्रकाशित किया जाने वाला स्मृतिग्रंथ भारत की उपलब्धियों को केवल सूचीबद्ध नही करेगा, बल्कि उसमें समाहित भावना, समर्पण और विचारधारा को भी उजागर करेगा। यह प्रयास देश के लिए प्रेरणास्रोत बनेगा।

मैं इस अभिनव प्रकाशन के लिए आयोजकों को शुभकामनाएं देता हूं और विश्वास करता हूं कि यह पुस्तक आने वाली पीढ़ियों को भारत के नवोदय की प्रेरणादायी गाथा के रूप में मार्गदर्शन प्रदान करेगी।

(आचार्य देवव्रत)

राजेंद्र विश्वनाथ आर्लेकर
राज्यपाल, केरल
RAJENDRA VISHWANATH ARLEKAR
GOVERNOR OF KERALA

सत्यमेव जयते

രാജേന്ദ്ര വിശ്വനാഥ് ആർലേക്കർ
ഗവർണ്ണർ, കേരളം

26 July 2025

MESSAGE

Glad to note that M/s. Gyan Books (P) Ltd., is bringing out a commemorative on 11 years of Modi Government's achievement. The past eleven years, under the visionary leadership of Hon'ble Prime Minister **Shri Narendra Modi**, India has witnessed a remarkable transformation rooted in good governance, inclusive development, and national resurgence. From financial inclusion to infrastructure expansion, and from global diplomacy to digital empowerment, the government's initiatives have touched every aspect of our collective progress. These years reflect a determined journey towards a self-reliant, confident, and resurgent India.

I commend Gyan Books Pvt. Ltd. for chronicling this significant journey, and I am confident that this publication will serve as a valuable reference for citizens, scholars, and policymakers alike.

Rajendra Vishwanath Arlekar

KERALA RAJ BHAVAN
THIRUVANANTHAPURAM-695 099
Tel : 0471-2721100, Fax : 0471-2720266, Email : keralagovernor@gmail.com

Introduction

For me, book publishing has never been merely a business—it has been a profession and a lifelong commitment. For more than three decades, I have had the privilege of working closely with the education industry and intellectual community of this country. Unlike commercial enterprises, our work has always been dependent on the wisdom, scholarship, and insights of professionals—vice-chancellors, professors, researchers, bureaucrats, political leaders, and activists—who regularly enrich us with their knowledge. Meeting such minds not only informs us but also creates the sense that we too are part of this intellectual journey, acquiring skills and perspectives through constant dialogue. Over the years, we have published works of national political leaders, seasoned bureaucrats, grassroots activists, and academic scholars. These authors do not belong to a single category, and precisely because of this diversity, our work has given us access to a wide spectrum of thought—political, social, cultural, and educational.

In the last three decades I have witnessed many shifts in India's social and political development, but the past decade stands out as especially transformative. At first, I wondered whether this was simply my own impression or whether it reflected the sentiment of the nation as a whole. To explore this question, I turned to higher educational institutions, the first step where young minds begin shaping their futures and where government policies are critically examined. I reached out to vice-chancellors across the country, and forty of them responded, sharing their views on the eleven-year journey of Prime Minister Modi's government. Their contributions, grounded in academic rigour and institutional experience, form the core of this book.

Modi's Leadership and Governance

Several contributors situate Modi's rise in the broader history of modern India. Prof. Nagaraj Ramrao, in *"The Ascent of Narendra Modi: A Transformational Journey Since 2014"*, highlights how 2014 marked a turning point in India's governance culture. Dr. Priyesh P. Gandhi, in *"An Epoch of Transformation"*, views Modi's tenure as a period of decisive leadership that redefined India's policy framework. Prof. Abhijit Dutta, in *"A Decade of Transformation"*, describes how reforms in economy, governance, and culture have reshaped India's trajectory.

Dr. Hidam Ajit Meetei and Bhavana Devi Tekcham, in *"Chronicling 11 Years of the Narendra Modi Government"*, document the key policy reforms and welfare initiatives—from Digital India to Atmanirbhar Bharat—that transformed service delivery and institutional efficiency. Er. Kordor Lamare, in *"Views, Experiences and Key Initiatives"*, underlines how Swachh Bharat, Make in India, and NITI Aayog symbolise Modi's mission-driven approach. Prof. Madan Mohan Goel, in *"A Needonomics Analysis of the Modi Era"*, frames these reforms through the lens of ethical economics, showing how transparency and efficiency became cornerstones of governance.

Dr. Naresh Kumar Tiwari, in *"Narendra Modi: A Leader with a Humanitarian Soul"*, reminds us that beyond policy, Modi's leadership is shaped by empathy and service. His humanitarian outlook—visible during natural disasters and in welfare outreach—remains central to his political persona.

Economic Transformation and Self-Reliance

The economy forms a recurring theme across essays. Prof. Raj Kumar Kothari, in *"PM Modi's Economic Reforms"*, analyses how GST, IBC, and Start-up India formalised and energised the economy. Prof. Rajeev Bhardwaj adds that growth and fiscal prudence went hand in hand, enabling India to withstand global crises. Dr. Radha Krishan Dhiman interprets economic reforms as laying foundations for inclusive prosperity, while Prof. Santosh Kumar Tripathy emphasises Modi's success in integrating economic vision with grassroots development.

Contributors also highlight initiatives like Make in India, PLI, and Atmanirbhar Bharat as central to India's manufacturing revival. Supplementing their views, we must also recall bold steps like demonetisation (2016), corporate tax reforms (2019), and the National Infrastructure Pipeline, all of which underscored Modi's ambition for a self-reliant economy.

Education and Knowledge Reforms

Education is the single largest theme in this volume, reflecting its importance for *Viksit Bharat @ 2047*. Dr. Amit Ganatra, in *"Transforming India's Education Landscape"*, foregrounds NEP 2020, research innovation, and industry-academia ties. Prof. Manpreet Singh Manna also explores this theme, seeing the decade as one of infinite possibilities in higher education. Dr. Krishnan Chalil, in *"Revolutionising Higher Education"*, details expansion of IITs, IIMs, AIIMS, and digital platforms.

Prof. K. Prathapan, in *"Reforms and Revolutions in HEIs"*, examines autonomy, accreditation, and digitalisation. Prof. Ankur Kulkarni, in *"Education with a Focus on IKS and NEP 2020"*, stresses integration of Indian Knowledge Systems with global pedagogy. Prof. K. K. Aggarwal, in *"Viksit Bharat @ 2047 via Education"*, projects education as the backbone of India's future development.

Dr. Tankeshwar Kumar, in *"A Visionary Leader Transforming India through Analytical Power"*, highlights research reforms like the **Anusandhan National Research Foundation.** Dr. Rajeev Manhas, in *"Opening New Windows to Knowledge Access"*, shows how digital platforms democratised education. Prof. Manabendra Dutta Choudhury and Dhanawantari L. Singha, in *"NEP 2020: Transforming Human Resources"*, argue that the policy will harness India's demographic dividend.

Prof. Javed Musarrat, in *"Transformative Governance: A Perspective on Educational Reforms"*, situates NEP within national development, while Dr. J. M. Vyas, in *"Narendra Modi Ji: Architect of Forensic Transformation"*, explains how forensic sciences and new technologies in education expanded under Modi. Dr. Jayanthi V and Dr. K. Satyanarayan Reddy both emphasise the need for skill-based learning and research-driven reforms.

Together, these chapters confirm that NEP 2020 is not simply an academic reform but a civilisational reset in how India views knowledge and its role in nation-building.

Social Welfare and Women-Led Development

The Modi era has seen social welfare expand in scale and scope. Prof. Som Nath Sachdeva outlines how financial inclusion and DBT changed state-citizen relations. Dr. N. Vani Shree examines PMAY, Ujjwala, and Ayushman Bharat as game-changers in social equity. Prof. Surender Kashyap highlights Ayushman Bharat's impact on healthcare. Ms. Rajeswari H, in her piece, emphasises rural empowerment schemes and their role in bridging social divides.

A special focus has been women-led development. Anusha C. Koti, in *"A Decade of Dignity and Self-Reliant Bharat"*, tracks the journey from Beti Bachao, Beti Padhao to Lakhpati Didi and Drone Didi. Prof. Rajul K. Gajjar underscores how women-centric schemes positioned women not just as beneficiaries but as leaders in economic and social life. The **Women's Reservation Bill (2023)** further institutionalised this shift.

Culture, Identity, and Civilisational Revival

Prof. Narasingha Charan Panda, in *"Bharatiya Chetanā and the Decade of Dharma"*, interprets Modi's tenure as a cultural awakening rooted in heritage. Dr. Shyam Sundar Rath expands on this, linking cultural policy with national identity. Prof. Debashis Bandyopadhyay highlights how Modi's cultural politics blends modernity with ancient values

This cultural reassertion is visible in projects like the **Kashi Vishwanath Corridor**, the **Ram Mandir at Ayodhya,** and recognition of **International Yoga Day.** The **abrogation of Article 370** and the **Citizenship Amendment Act** (**CAA**) symbolise decisive moves in redefining the national identity, though not without debate.

Sports, Health, and Youth

Prof. Sudhir Kumar Sharma, in *"11 Years of Achievements in Sports"*, showcases how initiatives like **Khelo India** and the **Fit India Movement** built sporting culture. Dr. Mohammad Samir Hussain adds that sports are now tied to diplomacy and employment. Dr. Radha Krishan Dhiman notes how youth policies complemented these efforts.

Healthcare receives attention in Prof. Surender Kashyap's and Prof. Rajeev Bhardwaj's chapters, which highlight Ayushman Bharat and pandemic management. Together, they show that public health has become a defining feature of Modi's governance.

Defence, Security, and Global Standing

India's global position under Modi is another recurring theme. Lt. Gen. Konsam Himalay Singh, in *"Eleven Years of Modi, As I Experienced It"*, describes a resurgence of national pride and strategic clarity. Hon'ble Lt. Gen. K. T. Parnaik highlights defence reforms and modernisation. Prof. K. P. Yadav underlines Modi's foreign policy as balancing assertiveness with humanitarianism.

Contributors note achievements like India's G20 Presidency, Vaccine Maitri, and leadership in the International Solar Alliance. Defence reforms, higher FDI in defence, and border infrastructure were part of making India more secure and globally respected.

Challenges and the Road Ahead

While celebrating achievements, contributors also acknowledge challenges. Unemployment, agrarian unrest, and social cohesion remain areas requiring sustained focus. The **farm laws (2020–21)** and their repeal symbolise both boldness and responsiveness. As **Prof. Rajeev Bhardwaj** and **Prof. Santosh Tripathy** note, India has made huge strides but must continue to balance growth with equity.

Conclusion

This volume brings together forty-one contributors who collectively provide a panoramic view of the Modi era. Those who explored governance and leadership—Prof. Nagaraj Ramrao, Dr. Priyesh P. Gandhi, Prof. Abhijit Dutta, Dr. Hidam Ajit Meetei and Bhavana Devi Tekcham, Er. Kordor Lamare, Prof. Madan Mohan Goel, and Dr. Naresh Kumar Tiwari—trace how Modi transformed statecraft with vision, ethics, and a humanitarian soul.

Contributors focusing on the economy—Prof. Raj Kumar Kothari, Prof. Rajeev Bhardwaj, Dr. Radha Krishan Dhiman, and Prof. Santosh Kumar Tripathy—analyse reforms such as GST, IBC, and Start-up India, while noting the balance between growth and inclusivity.

Education forms the largest cluster, with Dr. Amit

Ganatra, Prof. Manpreet Singh Manna, Dr. Krishnan Chalil, Prof. K. Prathapan, Prof. Ankur Kulkarni, Prof. K. K. Aggarwal, Dr. Tankeshwar Kumar, Dr. Rajeev Manhas, Prof. Manabendra Dutta Choudhury, Prof. Javed Musarrat, Dr. J. M. Vyas, Dr. Jayanthi V, and Dr. K. Satyanarayan Reddy all reflecting on NEP 2020, research reforms, knowledge access, and the expansion of higher education.

Social equity and women-led development are addressed by Prof. Som Nath Sachdeva, Dr. N. Vani Shree, Prof. Surender Kashyap, Ms. Rajeswari H, Prof. Rajul K. Gajjar, and Anusha C. Koti, who together highlight health, financial inclusion, and the new role of women as leaders in development.

The cultural dimension is explored by Prof. Narasingha Charan Panda, Dr. Shyam Sundar Rath, and Prof. Debashis Bandyopadhyay, who interpret Modi's decade as a revival of India's civilisational identity. Prof. Sudhir Kumar Sharma and Dr. Mohammad Samir Hussain highlight sports as an instrument of national pride and youth empowerment. Healthcare reforms are emphasised by Prof. Surender Kashyap and Prof. Rajeev Bhardwaj, who see Ayushman Bharat as a turning point.

Finally, contributors like Lt. Gen. Konsam Himalay Singh, Hon'ble Lt. Gen. K. T. Parnaik, and Prof. K. P. Yadav examine India's strengthened defence posture and assertive foreign policy, situating the Modi era within a rising global India.

Together, these voices construct a narrative of governance, economy, education, welfare, culture, defence, and diplomacy—all tied to the vision of *Viksit Bharat 2047*. They recognise achievements but also note persisting challenges, from unemployment to social cohesion.

As India enters *Amrit Kaal*, these eleven years may be remembered as the foundation of a resurgent nation—charting the path from aspiration to achievement, from empowerment to leadership, from governance to nation-building. This book, by giving space to India's intellectuals, captures not only the government's record but also the pulse of the nation itself.

★★★

As the contributors come from diverse categories—vice-chancellors, professors, and scholars—it was not feasible to follow a formal protocol in sequencing their articles. To ensure fairness and neutrality, the articles have been arranged in alphabetical order of contributors' names, giving equal space and respect to every voice.

1

How Narendra Modi's Government Reshaped India (2014–2025)

Prof. Abhijit Dutta[1]

Since coming to power in 2014, Prime Minister Narendra Modi's administration has driven transformative reforms across India's education, infrastructure, economy, and cultural preservation sectors. Marked by bold policy overhauls, a push for digital empowerment, and a vision of Atmanirbhar Bharat (self-reliant India), this eleven-year journey has witnessed some of the most sweeping changes in the country's recent history.

Education Overhaul: The National Education Policy 2020 and Beyond

The National Education Policy (NEP) 2020 is perhaps the crown jewel of the government's education reforms, marking a historic revamp after 34 years. It replaced the old 10+2 structure with a more developmentally aligned 5+3+3+4 system, introduced multilingual education with textbooks in 13 regional languages, and shifted focus from rote learning to experiential and vocational training starting as early as Grade 6.

The government's push for digital education has been equally robust. The DIKSHA platform today hosts over 3.6 lakh

1. Vice Chancellor (Officiating), Sikkim University.

e-content resources in 133 languages, while PM eVidya enabled remote learning for more than 250 million students during the COVID-19 pandemic. Connectivity through BharatNet aims to link all government secondary schools with high-speed broadband, fostering digital inclusion even in rural areas.

Higher education infrastructure has expanded rapidly under Modi's tenure:

Institution Type	2014 Count	2024 Count
IITs	16	23
IIMs	13	20
Universities	723	1,213
Medical Colleges	499 (FY19)	780 (FY25)

Over 110,000 medical seats have been added, with more on the horizon. The PM Research Fellowship also supports 10,000 bright minds pursuing advanced research at premier institutes.

Inclusion and equity remain priorities. Schemes like Beti Bachao Beti Padhao and Kasturba Gandhi Balika Vidyalaya bolster girl child education, while dropout rates at the secondary level dropped from 21% in 2013–14 to 13% in 2021–22. The Gross Enrollment Ratio for women in higher education rose by 32% over the same period.

Indicator	2013–14	2021–22
Secondary School Dropout Rate (%)	21	13
GER Women in Higher Education (%)	26.5	35

Reviving Ancient Wisdom: India's Traditional Knowledge Goes Digital

The government has invested heavily in preserving and modernizing India's rich traditional knowledge systems. The Traditional Knowledge Digital Library (TKDL) digitizes over 400,000 formulations from Ayurveda, Unani, Siddha, and Yoga, making them accessible in five global languages. Its 2022 expansion now allows researchers and businesses beyond patent offices to access this treasure trove.

In April 2022, the World Health Organisation established its first Global Centre for Traditional Medicine in India, highlighting the country's leadership in this field.

Innovations like Ayurgenomics use artificial intelligence (AI) to merge ancient healing practices with modern science — AI-powered diagnostics now assist in pulse reading and tongue analysis, ushering Ayurveda into the 21st century.

The Science and Heritage Research Initiative (SHRI) further promotes integrating ancient manuscripts and monuments—over 5 million of them—with modern scientific research, preserving India's cultural legacy while encouraging innovation.

Skill Development and Employment: Building a Future-Ready Workforce

Skilling initiatives have trained millions. The Pradhan Mantri Kaushal Vikas Yojana (PMKVY) has upskilled over 16.3 million youth in sectors ranging from digital literacy to problem-solving. Complementing this is the Employment Linked Incentive Scheme (ELI), targeting 20 million new jobs in two years, especially in MSMEs.

To provide world-class training, five National Centres of Excellence have been established, collaborating with global experts.

Infrastructure Boom: Parliament, Kartavya Path, and Railways

- India's infrastructure landscape has been transformed with iconic projects:
- The **new Parliament building,** inaugurated in 2023, is a symbol of modern India's democratic values, equipped with cutting-edge technology and sustainable architecture.

The **Kartavya Path** (formerly Rajpath) was revamped into a grand ceremonial boulevard, reflecting the nation's pride and hosting key national events.

Railways have witnessed unprecedented growth, especially in connectivity to strategic regions. The introduction of the **Vande Bharat Express,** India's semi-high-speed train, has revolutionised rail travel with faster, safer, and more comfortable journeys.

Crucially, railway projects in **Kashmir** (Udhampur-Srinagar-Baramulla line) are operational, fostering integration and economic activity in the sensitive region. Meanwhile, the ambitious railway line linking **Sikkim** with the broader network is progressing steadily.

Railway Initiative	Key Details
Vande Bharat Express	Semi-high-speed trains; enhanced speed & safety
Kashmir Rail Connectivity	Udhampur-Srinagar-Baramulla line operational
Sikkim Railway Project	Under construction; connects Sikkim with rest of India
Railway Electrification	Over 70% route electrified by 2024

Budget and Economic Reform: Steering Growth and Inclusion

The government's budgetary commitment to education grew substantially from ₹ 68,728 crore in 2014 to ₹ 1,12,899 crore in 2024, underlining a priority on human capital development.

Year	Education Budget (₹ Crore)
2014	68,728
2024	1,12,899

Major economic reforms have restructured India's economy:

- The **Goods and Services Tax (GST)** unified indirect taxes across states, simplifying compliance.

- The **Pradhan Mantri Jan Dhan Yojana** has promoted financial inclusion, opening over 400 million bank accounts.
- The **Insolvency and Bankruptcy Code (IBC)** streamlined corporate debt resolution, improving credit discipline.

Other Flagship Programmes: Digital India, Make in India, Ayushman Bharat, and Atmanirbhar Bharat

- **Digital India,** launched in 2015, has brought broadband connectivity to rural areas and transformed public service delivery.
- **Make in India** aims to position the country as a global manufacturing hub, attracting investment and creating jobs in electronics, textiles, and more.
- **Ayushman Bharat** provides health insurance coverage of ₹ 5 lakh per family, benefiting over 50 crore citizens.
- The **Atmanirbhar Bharat Abhiyan**, introduced amid the COVID-19 pandemic, drives self-reliance by boosting local manufacturing and reducing imports.

Conclusion: Visible Progress, Hard Work, and a New India

Eleven years into Narendra Modi's tenure, the visible transformation across India is undeniable. The government's holistic approach—integrating technology, heritage, infrastructure, and inclusive policies—has reshaped the country's development narrative.

The NEP 2020 and digital education platforms are empowering millions of students. The preservation and digitization of traditional knowledge have blended cultural pride with cutting-edge innovation. Infrastructure projects, from the new Parliament and Kartavya Path to expanded railway networks in Kashmir and Sikkim, symbolize India's march toward modernity and integration.

Economic reforms have fortified the country's financial architecture while creating jobs and promoting entrepreneurship. Healthcare initiatives like Ayushman Bharat have enhanced wellbeing for tens of millions.

Behind these achievements lies immense hard work by policymakers, educators, scientists, and citizens alike. Their dedication has made the ambitious vision of a self-reliant, prosperous India a reality on the ground.

As the nation looks ahead, these reforms lay a strong foundation for India's emergence as a global knowledge and innovation leader—culturally rooted, digitally empowered, and inclusive of all its people.

Over the past eleven years, the Narendra Modi administration has embarked on an ambitious journey of transformation, reshaping India's educational framework, infrastructure, traditional knowledge systems, and economic landscape. These comprehensive reforms are not merely policies on paper but represent the culmination of relentless dedication, visionary leadership, and collaborative efforts across various levels of government and society. The hard work invested by countless policymakers, educators, scientists, and frontline workers has translated into tangible outcomes that are visible in every corner of the country.

From the classrooms enriched by the National Education Policy 2020 and digital learning platforms to the medical colleges nurturing thousands of healthcare professionals, India's human capital is being systematically empowered to meet the demands of a rapidly changing world. The digitization of ancient wisdom and the fusion of science with heritage underscore a respect for India's cultural roots while embracing the future.

Infrastructure development, particularly in railways, reflects a nation moving towards enhanced connectivity and economic integration. Projects in strategic regions like Kashmir and Sikkim, alongside the introduction of cutting-edge trains such as the Vande Bharat Express, demonstrate India's commitment to modernity and inclusivity. The inauguration of the new Parliament building and the beautification of Kartavya Path symbolize a nation proud of its democratic ethos and rich heritage.

Economic reforms such as the GST, financial inclusion schemes, and employment-linked incentives have fostered a more resilient and formalised economy, facilitating growth and opportunity for millions. Programmes like Ayushman Bharat have brought healthcare within the reach of millions, alleviating financial distress and improving quality of life.

Together, these efforts have propelled India onto a path of visible and sustainable national development. Cities are becoming smarter, rural areas better connected, youth better skilled, and citizens more digitally empowered. This progress reflects not just policy success but the collective spirit and resilience of the Indian people.

As India continues this upward trajectory, the Modi government's eleven years in office stand as a testament to how vision, perseverance, and inclusive governance can foster a transformed nation. The reforms laid down are the foundation stones for a future where India is not only self-reliant but also a global leader in innovation, culture, and sustainable development. The journey continues, driven by the promise of a prosperous and equitable India for generations to come.

References

Ayushman Bharat. (n.d.). Retrieved July 25, 2025, from https://ayushmanbharat.mp.gov.in/

Budget 2025-2026: Speech of Nirmala Sitharaman, Ministry of Finance. (2025, January 2). India. Ministry of Finance. https://www.indiabudget.gov.in/doc/budget_speech.pdf

Department of Financial Services. (2021). Jan Dhan Yojana Progress Report. Government of India.

Digital India: MeitY, Government of India. (n.d.). Retrieved July 25, 2025, from https://www.digitalindia.gov.in/

Employment Linked Incentive Scheme 2025: Eligibility, Benefits, and How to Apply Online - सरकारी योजना. (2025, July 2). https://sarkariyojana.com/employment-linked-incentive-scheme/

Government of India. (2018). GST Year-End Review (No. Annual Report).

India's AI-Powered Ayurveda Revolution: A Global Milestone. (2025, July 20). Global Education News. https://globaleducationnews.org/indias-ai-powered-ayurveda-revolution-a-global-milestone/

L&T EduTech. (2023, July 30). Digital Empowerment & Capacity Building in Education. 2nd Akhil Bharatiya Shiksha Samagam, New Delhi.

Make In India. (n.d.). Retrieved July 25, 2025, from https://www.makeinindia.com/

Ministry of Corporate Affairs. (2020). IBC Impact Analysis.

National Centres Of Excellence For Skilling 2024—IMPRI Impact And Policy Research Institute. (n.d.). Retrieved July 25, 2025, from https://www.impriindia.com/insights/national-centres-of-excellence-for-skilling/

National Education Policy 2020. (2020). [Policy]. Government of India. https://www.education.gov.in/sites/upload_files/mhrd/files/NEP_Final_English.pdf

NITI Aayog. (2025). Expanding Quality Higher Education through States and State Public Universities [Policy Report]. NITI Aayog. https://www.niti.gov.in/sites/default/files/2025-02/Expanding-Quality-Higher-Education-through-SPUs.pdf

Pradhan Mantri Kaushal Vikas Yojana| National Portal of India. (n.d.). Retrieved July 25, 2025, from https://www.india.gov.in/spotlight/pradhan-mantri-kaushal-vikas-yojana#tab=tab-1

Science and Heritage Research Initiative (SHRI) | Department Of Science & Technology. (n.d.). Retrieved July 25, 2025, from https://dst.gov.in/science-and-heritage-research-initiative-shri

Self-reliant India (Aatm Nirbhar Bharat Abhiyan) | IBEF. (n.d.). India Brand Equity Foundation. Retrieved July 25, 2025, from https://www.ibef.org/government-schemes/self-reliant-india-aatm-nirbhar-bharat-abhiyan

Traditional Knowledge Digital Library Unit (TKDL) | Council of Scientific & Industrial Research. (n.d.). Retrieved July 25, 2025, from https://www.csir.res.in/en/documents/tkdl

University of Lucknow, Singh, D., & Mishra, R. S. (2023). Equity and Inclusion in Indian Education: Constitutional Principles and NEP 2020 Approaches. BSSS Journal of Education, 12(01), 128–139. https://doi.org/10.51767/je1208

WHO Global Traditional Medicine Centre. (n.d.). Retrieved July 25, 2025, from https://www.who.int/teams/who-global-traditional-medicine-centre/over-view

2

Transforming India's Education Landscape: The Decade of Revolutionary Reforms

Dr. Amit Ganatra[1]

This piece will provide an authoritative analysis of three pivotal areas where policy interventions have created lasting impact:

1. **The National Education Policy 2020: Redefining Indian Academia**

   Examining how this visionary framework has:

   - Liberated our education system from colonial constraints
   - Fostered multidisciplinary learning ecosystems
   - Positioned India as a global education destination through internationalisation

2. **Bridging the Skills Gap: Academia-Industry Convergence** Detailing successful models of:

   - Skill-integrated degree programmes producing job-ready graduates
   - Corporate partnerships enhancing employability

1. Provost, Parul University, Vadodara, Gujarat 390716.

- Our university's hands-on experience implementing these initiatives

3. **Research & Innovation: Building an Atmanirbhar Bharat** Highlighting:
   - The exponential growth in academic patents and startups
   - How research funding reforms are fueling innovation
   - Inspiring stories from our student entrepreneur community

The article will blend rigorous policy analysis with concrete examples from our institutional experience at Parul University, supported by verifiable data on enrollment growth, placement statistics, and research output. I will particularly emphasize how these reforms are creating a new generation of Indian youth who combine traditional values with global competencies.

I understand the importance of meeting your publication timeline for the August 15, 2025 release. Please share any specific formatting guidelines or submission deadlines to ensure my contribution aligns perfectly with your editorial vision. Having reviewed your previous work on PM Modi's governance philosophy, I'm confident this volume will similarly become an invaluable resource for understanding India's development narrative.

I look forward to collaborating on this meaningful project that celebrates our nation's progress while inspiring future achievements.

3

Narendra Modi government (2014–2025) in the realm of education, with a special focus on IKS and NEP 2020

Prof. (Dr.) Ankur Kulkarni[1]

Under the visionary leadership of Hon'ble Prime Minister Narendra Modi Ji, the Indian education sector has witnessed a wave of transformative reforms designed to prepare the nation's youth for the challenges of the 21st century while staying deeply rooted in India's timeless wisdom. These initiatives aim not only to strengthen classrooms but also to shape the future of the nation through its learners. Education under Modi Ji's leadership is envisioned as more than academic achievement, it is about nurturing complete human beings. The reforms focus on making learning holistic, multidisciplinary, and skill-oriented, so that students emerge as confident, creative, and compassionate individuals ready to lead meaningful lives.

A strong emphasis has been placed on ensuring that education reaches every corner of India from urban cities to rural villages. The government's initiatives are designed to reduce inequalities, provide opportunities to marginalised groups, and create an

1. Vice Chancellor- SAGE University, Indore aenkurr@gmail.com

education system that is inclusive, affordable, and accessible to all. Recognizing the evolving global economy, Modi Ji's policies promote skill-based learning, vocational training, and entrepreneurship. By encouraging innovation and hands-on experience, these reforms empower students to not only seek.

Landmark Policy Reform: NEP 2020

The National Education Policy (NEP) 2020 stands as one of the most transformative reforms in the history of Indian education introduced after more than three decades. It is not merely a policy document, but a vision for reshaping the future of learning in India, placing the learner at the very heart of education. The NEP 2020 is built on five core principles i.e. access, equity, quality, affordability, and accountability ensuring that every child, regardless of background, has the opportunity to learn, grow, and thrive. Unlike traditional systems that focused heavily on exams and rote memorisation, this policy emphasizes conceptual understanding, curiosity-driven exploration, and lifelong learning.

One of the boldest steps of NEP is its move away from rigid subject silos. Students now have the freedom to choose subjects across streams, blending arts, science, and vocational learning based on their interests. This multidisciplinary approach opens doors for creativity, innovation, and holistic development. The policy also recognizes the importance of a child's roots, emphasizing early education in the mother tongue or regional language, helping young learners connect more deeply with knowledge while feeling emotionally secure in the classroom.

Replacing the old 10+2 system, the 5+3+3+4 structure is a visionary framework that focuses on foundational learning in the early years. By prioritizing play-based, activity-based, and discovery-based education, NEP ensures that children build strong learning habits from the very beginning. Recognizing the digital age, NEP 2020 integrates technology as a key enabler. Platforms like DIKSHA, PM e-VIDYA, SWAYAM, SWAYAM Prabha, and NDEAR (National Digital Education Architecture) ensure that learning resources are accessible to all, from remote villages to metropolitan cities. NEP acknowledges that teachers are the backbone of education. To support their growth, the National Professional Standards for Teachers (NPST) was introduced, setting benchmarks for teacher training, professional development, and continuous learning. By empowering teachers, the policy ensures students receive guidance not just as learners, but as future citizens and leaders.

Promotion of Indian Knowledge Systems (IKS)

One of the most remarkable initiatives under the leadership of Hon'ble Prime Minister Narendra Modi Ji has been the revival and promotion of Indian Knowledge Systems (IKS) a sincere effort to reconnect education with the intellectual, cultural, and spiritual roots of India. This reform is not about looking back nostalgically, but about carrying timeless wisdom forward into the future in a way that is relevant, meaningful, and empowering for today's youth.

The government has established a dedicated IKS Division under AICTE, signaling a strong commitment to integrating India's rich heritage into the fabric of modern education. Through this initiative, students are not only introduced to Sanskrit, Vedic sciences, Ayurveda, Yoga, Indian logic, and traditional knowledge streams, but also encouraged to appreciate their practical applications in contemporary life from wellness and sustainable living to holistic science and innovation.

The inclusion of Indian heritage, epics, and cultural narratives in curricula has brought new dimensions of identity and pride among learners. By reintroducing these elements in schools and universities, education becomes a medium for strengthening cultural roots while nurturing global citizens.

Dedicated IKS Centers have been established in leading insti-tutions like IITs, NITs, and central universities, creating platforms for research, documentation, and dissemination of traditional knowledge. These centers foster dialogue between ancient wisdom and modern science, ensuring students develop a balanced worldview—rooted in tradition, yet responsive to contemporary challenges.

At its heart, the IKS initiative is about humanizing education reminding young learners that education is not just about employability, but also about identity, values, and meaning. It empowers them to draw strength from India's timeless knowledge while contributing confidently to global innovation and progress.

Institutional and Policy Reforms

Under the leadership of Hon'ble Prime Minister Narendra Modi Ji, India's education landscape has been undergoing landmark institutional and policy reforms. These reforms are not just structural changes on paper, but a determined effort to make education more student-centric, research-driven, globally competitive, and deeply humane. A visionary step has been the proposal of the Higher Education Commission of India (HECI) a single, overarching regulator to replace bodies like UGC, AICTE, and NCTE. This reform simplifies governance, reduces duplication, and ensures that quality, accountability, and innovation become the benchmarks of higher education.

The government has envisioned Multidisciplinary Education and Research Universities (MERUs), modeled on the world's best institutions. These MERUs aim to create spaces where innovation, creativity, and multidisciplinary collaboration thrive, ensuring that Indian universities can stand proudly among global leaders. Recognizing that research is the heart of progress, the National Research Foundation has been set up with a ₹ 50,000+ crore funding plan. This initiative supports quality research across disciplines, empowering students, faculty, and institutions to solve India's problems while contributing to global knowledge.

For younger learners, the Foundational Literacy and Numeracy Mission (NIPUN Bharat) aims to achieve universal literacy and numeracy by Grade 3 laying a strong educational foundation for every child. The Samagra Shiksha Abhiyan integrates earlier schemes (SSA, RMSA, and Teacher Education) to ensure holistic development of schools, covering infrastructure, teacher training, and inclusive education.

To move beyond rote memorisation, the government introduced PARAKH (Performance Assessment, Review, and Analysis of Knowledge for Holistic Development) a transformative assessment framework under NEP. PARAKH emphasizes conceptual learning, critical thinking, and holistic development over marks and grades.

Through NIRF Rankings and institutional accreditation reforms, universities and colleges are now encouraged to strive for excellence, transparency, and global competitiveness. Alongside, major emphasis is being placed on faculty development, academic leadership training, and integration of AI and digital tools in education making teachers and institutions future-ready.

Skill Development and Innovation

In today's rapidly changing world, education cannot end in the classroom, it must prepare students to think, create, and lead. Recognizing this, the Government of India under Hon'ble Prime Minister Narendra Modi Ji's leadership has placed strong emphasis on skill development, innovation, and entrepreneurship, ensuring that the nation's youth are not just job seekers but job creators and problem- solvers.

Through the Skill India Mission and the National Apprenticeship Promotion Scheme (NAPS), millions of young

Indians are being equipped with industry-relevant skills. These programmes make students more employable, bridge the gap between classroom knowledge and workplace requirements, and provide real-world exposure through hands-on apprenticeships.

The Atal Innovation Mission (AIM) has ignited the spirit of creativity and discovery in young learners. By establishing Atal Tinkering Labs in schools and Atal Incubation Centres in higher education institutions, AIM nurtures curiosity, problem-solving, and innovation from an early age. Children and youth are encouraged to experiment, explore, and innovate, making learning both practical and exciting.

Under the Start-Up India Initiative, incubation centres have been launched across universities and colleges to support student-led start-ups. These centres provide mentorship, funding opportunities, and infrastructure, enabling students to transform their ideas into scalable ventures. This reform has turned campuses into hubs of entrepreneurship, where creativity is not only appreciated but actively supported. The reforms also bring vocational training into the mainstream of school education, ensuring that practical life skills such as digital literacy, financial management, and technical know-how become part of a student's journey. By doing so, the system fosters self-reliance, adaptability, and an entrepreneurial mindset, preparing the youth for the demands of the 21st-century economy.

Internationalisation and Collaboration

In an era where knowledge knows no borders, India is stepping forward as a global hub of education, innovation, and cultural exchange. Under the vision of Hon'ble Prime Minister Narendra Modi Ji's government, internationalisation has become a cornerstone of educational reform aimed at making Indian institutions more vibrant, competitive, and globally relevant. The Study in India Programme has been launched to attract students from across the globe to Indian universities. By showcasing India's world-class academic programmes, affordable education, rich culture, and heritage of knowledge, the initiative has turned India into a preferred destination for global learners. Foreign students not only gain education but also experience India's diverse traditions, languages, and values, making their stay a holistic journey of learning and life.

Through Dual Degree, Joint Degree, and Twinning Programmes with leading global universities, Indian students now enjoy opportunities to study across borders without losing connection to their roots. These programmes provide international exposure, cross-cultural understanding, and diverse academic experiences, preparing students to compete and collaborate on a global stage. They also bring global faculty, expertise, and practices into Indian institutions, enriching the learning ecosystem.

The introduction of the National Institutional Ranking Framework (NIRF) has brought much-needed transparency, accountability, and healthy competition among Indian universities. Institutions are now motivated to improve quality in teaching, research, and innovation, while students and parents benefit from credible information to make informed choices.

4

A Decade of Dignity and Self-Reliant Bharat

Journey From Women Empowerment to Women-Led Development

Prof. Anusha C Koti[1]

Introduction

"*Empowered women empower the nation.*" This statement reflects the core of India's evolving development model. Women's empowerment focuses on providing women with access, rights, and opportunities—lifting barriers to their participation in society. Women-led development, however, goes a step further by positioning women as active leaders and decision-makers in economic, social, and political spheres. The Modi government's shift from empowerment to leadership marks a transformative approach, recognizing women not just as beneficiaries but as drivers of national progress. This article highlights the important initiatives of the Modi government in this journey towards women-led development.

Phase I - Foundations of Empowerment

The initial years of the Modi government laid a strong foundation for women's empowerment by focusing on access, dignity, and inclusion. The emphasis was on removing structural barriers that had long hindered women's participation in social and economic life.

1. Assistant Professor of Law at KLE Law College, Bengaluru

One of the earliest and most impactful initiatives was Beti Bachao, Beti Padhao, launched in 2015 to address the declining child sex ratio and promote the value of the girl child. It focused on generating awareness and improving the efficiency of welfare services for girls, particularly through education and healthcare. The Sex Ratio at Birth in India has improved by 12 points, rising from 918 to 930 in the last 10 years[1].

The Pradhan Mantri Ujjwala Yojana (PMUJ), launched in 2016, provided free LPG connections to over 10.33 crore women from below-poverty-line households[2]. It not only improved indoor air quality and health but also gave women greater freedom, dignity in the kitchen, and the ability to indulge in other core activities.

The Kishori Shakti Yojana, launched in 2000, played a vital role in addressing the needs of adolescent girls, particularly in rural and disadvantaged areas. It focused on girls aged 11 to 18; the scheme aimed to improve their nutritional and health status, promote awareness about social and legal rights, and equip them with life skills. By fostering education, hygiene, and self-confidence, it laid a strong foundation for women's empowerment from an early age, preparing them to become active participants in development.

Through the Swachh Bharat Mission, millions of toilets were constructed in rural areas, many of which were registered in the names of women. This promoted hygiene, security, and dignity, especially for women and girls.

---

1. Ministry of Women and Child Development, 'Empowering India's Daughter' (*PIB,* 21 January 2025) <https://www.pib.gov.in/PressReleasePage.aspx? PRID=2094929> accessed on 24th July 24 2025
2. Ministry of Petroleum and Natural Gas, 'Nine Years of Empowering Lives Through Clean Energy', (*PIB,* 30 April 2025) <https://www.pib.gov.in/PressNoteDetails.aspx?NoteId=154355&ModuleId=3> accessed on 24 July 2025

These schemes represent some of the most impactful initiatives focused on women's empowerment in the initial years of the Modi government. By addressing critical areas such as health, education, sanitation, and dignity, they enabled women to gain greater control over their lives. Collectively, they laid the foundation for economic participation, enhanced self-worth, and deeper social inclusion, setting the stage for a more transformative shift—one where women move from being empowered individuals to leaders in India's journey toward women-led development.

Phase II: Shift Toward Participation and Leadership (2018 Onwards)

The Modi government's policies have evolved from being women-centric, focused on welfare and protection, to actively promoting women-led development, where women are positioned as leaders of transformation. It is emphasized by the Prime Minister at the G20 Summit (2023) that Women-led development is a national and global priority. This shift is reflected in gender budgeting, ensuring public expenditure supports women's empowerment; digital skilling programmes that prepare women for the future economy; and enhanced access to capital through schemes like Mudra and Stand-Up India. Women are now envisioned not just as recipients of support but as agents of economic growth and social leadership.

The Lakhpati Didi Scheme (2024) empowered rural women through self-help groups (SHGs), promoting skill development and enabling them to earn ₹ 1 lakh annually through micro-enterprises such as tailoring, organic farming, or handicrafts, thereby transforming them into local entrepreneurs. The scheme has identified and nurtured 2.47 crore Potential Lakhpati Didi's (PLDs) across the country[1].

1. Government of India, 'Lakhpati Didi Scheme: A milestone in women's economic upliftment' (*PIB*, 29 August 2024) <https://www.pib.gov.

Under PM Awas Yojana, women were made mandatory co-owners or sole owners of houses built under the scheme. This provides women with a tangible asset, enhancing their economic security and social status within the family and community. Home ownership empowers women to participate more confidently in financial and legal decision-making. It also creates a sense of stability, encouraging women's involvement in livelihood activities and entrepreneurship. Overall, the scheme transforms women from passive beneficiaries to active stakeholders in development. As of 19 November 2024, 3.21 crore houses have been sanctioned, and 2.67 crore houses have been completed, significantly improving the living conditions of millions of rural families[1].

The Stand-Up India Scheme is a significant step toward women-led development, as it facilitates institutional credit to women entrepreneurs for launching greenfield enterprises. By ensuring that each bank branch supports at least one woman borrower, the scheme creates a widespread platform for women to become first-generation business owners. This not only fosters financial independence but also enables women to generate employment, especially in underserved rural and semi-urban areas. Importantly, it promotes leadership among SC/ST women, addressing both gender and social equity. Around 84% of the beneficiaries under Stand-Up India are women[2].

---

in/PressNoteDetails.aspx?NoteId=152064&ModuleId=3 >accessed on 1 August 2025.

1. Ministry of Rural Development, 'Pradhan Mantri Awas Yojana- Rural: Building a Better Future for Rural India', (*PIB,* 19 November 2024) <https://www.pib.gov.in/PressReleasePage.aspx?PRID=2074713> accessed on 1 August 2025.
2. Government of India, 'NARI SHAKTI: From Women Development to Women-led Development', (*PIB,* 6 March 2024) <*https://www.pib.gov.in/PressNoteDetails.aspx?NoteId=151861&ModuleId=3* > accessed on 1 August 2025.

Entrepreneurship helps women shift from job seekers to leaders of local economic growth.

These initiatives collectively represent a decisive shift toward women-led development, where women are no longer just participants but central agents of change. This inclusive approach not only uplifts individual lives but also strengthens the nation's path toward sustainable and equitable growth.

Conclusion

Over the last 10 years, the Modi government has steered a powerful transition from women's empowerment to women-led development, recognizing women not merely as recipients of welfare but as active architects of India's progress. Through targeted schemes in health, housing, finance, and entrepreneurship, women have gained dignity, assets, and leadership. This transformation aligns with Sustainable Development Goal 5 (Gender Equality) and complements international child-related commitments like the UN Convention on the Rights of the Child, by nurturing a generation of empowered girls and resilient communities. The shift reflects a long-term vision for an inclusive, equitable, and self-reliant Bharat by 2047.

5

Mr Modi: A Visionary *Karmayogi* in Action

A Select Review of 11 years of governance

Prof. (Dr.) Debashis Bandyopadhyay[1]

When the country overwhelmingly voted Mr Narendra Modi and the BJP government to power, the people were confident to find in their leader an honest, strong and visionary person who will save the country from the festering caste, creed and class-based politics and set it on a constructivist nationalist pathway. He will undo to the best of his ability the wrongs done to its sacred heritage and nationalist pride.

The first tangible change was felt in the work culture of the government and public sector services. A strict disciplinarian regime made services in this sector smooth, fast and transparent. Coupled with it was launched a bold drive towards overhaul of the economy that had for almost six decades since Independence been trudging through the sludge of graft and unaccounted for black money. Only six percent of the country's total population filed tax returns on the eve of Modi government's revolutionary move towards demonetization in 2016. Illicit cash were stashed away and money laundering was rampant, making the national exchequer and the country's GDP teeter and falter. With an

1. Vice Chancellor, Kalinga Institute of Social Sciences, Deemed University (KISS-DU), Bhubaneswar.

effective implementation of demonetization, the tax revenue increased by a whopping 25 percent in a single financial year of 2017-2018. Transparency of financial and social exchanges increased several times and direct transmission of benefits to clients was facilitated with the introduction of Aadhar and cashless digital transactions.

The iron man of our choice lived up to our expectations. He had the grit to settle for ever the Kashmir issue that pestered us for more than half a century since the country's Independence. In 1952, the promulgation of Article 370, that granted separate state autonomy to J& K, was a political misadventure. Ever since, the province's strategic status roiled the nation's body politic like a canker on a rose. In 2019, Mr Modi snipped off the canker and integrated J&K to the sovereign state of India by abrogating Article 370 by a voice vote in the Parliament.

Prior to 2014, terror strikes inside the Indian territory were borne with insipid lethargy. Only a gutsy resolve on the part of the Modi government in instances of Uri, Pulwama and Pahelgam showed how India should not only retaliate but aggressively decimate the terrorist hideouts and guerrilla enclaves even if they are harbored inside Pakistan. Between 2014 and 2024, the number of terrorist incidents in J & K declined to 2,242 from a total of 7,217 that took place between 2004 and 2014. Total deaths reduced by 70 percent, while the loss of civilian lives fell by 81% and military casualties dipped by 50 percent. The strategic design to contain terrorism was carefully supplemented by a ₹ 6,839 crore transformative initiative titled Vibrant Villages Programme II, aimed at turning India's border villages into model hubs of development and progress.

The Modi government's inclusive development plans in Naxal-hit areas have reduced the total affected districts from 126 to 6 in the span of eleven years. The government has pledged to eradicate the menace by 2026. The most significant example of transformation is Bastar, an erstwhile Naxalite hotbed, that once quailed under the eerie sounds of gunfire now rings with the perky sounds of school bells and the rhythmic tunes of *dhamsa* and *madal*. A much-awaited focus on security and law enforcement was finally laid. The Union Home Ministry took active measures to motivate and enliven the morale of the security personnel through direct interaction at the ground level. The tension that tormented the north-east provinces was allayed to a great extent and with the revival of a sense of unity with the Indian body polity the Prime Minister's vision of "Ek Bharat, Shrestha Bharat" cruised to fulfillment. With the introduction of the three New Criminal Laws in 1 July 2024, the judicial process was streamlined, trials expedited and justice speedily dispensed.

Modi ji showed the tremendous fortitude and courage to contest and win the Babri Masjid issue in the apex court. For how many years did the politicians feed on the communal vote bank under the guise of secularism? For how many years did they disregard the majoritarian cultural craving to see the reconstruction of the Ram Temple in Ayodhya that Babur's military commander Mir Baqui destroyed savagely in 1528? Mr Modi fulfilled our dream finally.

There was a nasty hue and cry when Modi went to inaugurate the Ayodhya temple: why should the country's PM officially offer obeisance to any religious deity? Ridiculous argument when we knew very well that we have voted to power a dispensation that had built its principles on a much-acclaimed nationalist text. Political shenanigans are similar to misadventures that breed scurvy bogeys for years to come. One such bogey was raised by detractors when Dr Rajendra Prasad, the first President of our country, decided to offer his prayers to Shiva in the reconstructed Somnath Temple in 1951. Almost every Indian child has read in middle school how many times

Sultan Mahmud of Ghazni had ravaged and looted the sacred precincts of Somnath.

The forward-looking approach was not only restricted to restoration of the country's architectural past but was translated into a holistic revival of the nation's identity amidst the changing world order. The country's education policy was revised. Today's students are the future architects of *vikshit* Bharat. On the one hand they should be inspired to take pride in the country's heritage and strength and on the other become equipped with the scientific and technological skills required for progress in a globalised world. The National Education Policy of 2020 was drafted and put into effect. For the first time since Independence a holistic and humanistic approach towards self-development and nation building was envisaged in the most effective way possible. The indigenous knowledge system was extricated from the discursive politics of Saidian orientalism and organized into a modular structure while a multi-disciplinary technique-intensive curricular framework was designed for capacity building and achieving a more recognizably international benchmark.

In keeping with the nation's *sanatani* principles of love and universal kinship, our Prime Minister engaged in an active role of consolidating regional and global relationships. In the 6th BIMSTEC (Bay of Bengal Initiative for Multi-Sectoral Technical and Economic Cooperation) Summit held in Thailand on 4 April this year, he rolled out a 21-point Action Plan to energize the collaboration between South and Southeast Asian countries. The constructive approach intended to build a secure and culturally united region laid primary emphasis on trade, digital economy, disaster management, space, security and youth engagement. In the view of planetary concerns of climate change and increasing natural calamities, India assumed a responsible global leadership in disaster management. It spearheaded the 42 country and 60 MNC Coalition for Disaster Resilient Infrastructure (CDRI). At the direction of Mr Modi NDRF teams were sent to earthquake-ravaged countries worldwide.

These proactive efforts for glocal peace and cooperation were launched in tandem with adopting measures to secure the country's political and economic sovereignty. Because of this rounded visionary outlook of Mr Modi the country in 11 years of his governance has grown the ability to turn around under any attempted external pressure and resist all forms of scorn and snigger. When the US tried to flood the Indian market with their mechanised farm products like grains, fruit, dairy and fish, at the peril of the poor Indian farmers, Mr Modi took a firm decision against it. Despite knowing that this might cause a backlash on Indo-US trade relations, our Prime Minister was patriotic enough to prioritize the interests of the poverty-stricken masses of the country by saving the domestic agri market from Trump's attempted capitalist depredations. The price for this nationalist stance was not insignificant: the US levied 25 percent tariff on Indian goods entering their market. The ordeal did not end there. When Mr Modi showed iron determination not to yield to Trump's diktat against India's readiness to purchase crude oil from Russia, the US slapped an additional 25 percent tariff on Indian exports to their country. This is not only unfortunate but a discriminatory tactic when compared with Trump's attitude to other south-Asian countries like China on the same issue.

Mr Modi, however, has a steely spine; he has endeavoured to build up the third largest and fastest growing economy of the world not for nothing. He will not bend to unjustified pressure or kowtow to hegemonic scowls: the west should have a feel of India's economic resilience and hardy endurance; it has emerged as a global power that hegemons cannot toy with or drub whenever they like. The Trump-Modi personal chemistry notwithstanding, our PM has played his economic and political cards well without sacrificing any space for negotiation with the 'big brother'.

Quite interestingly, however, the National Statistics Office (NSO) released the empirical proof of India's extraordinary growth rate amidst the brewing tariff tension. Steps taken by the Modi government to boost the farm sector and revive the manufacturing and services sectors have yielded unprecedented dividends: the GDP surged to an all time high of 7.8 % in the June quarter of the current fiscal year. This convincingly surpassed the Reserve Bank of India's projected estimate of 6.5% for the same period. The common people's average buying capacity, which is also a rough index of their financial well-being, registered a sharp increase. According to the NSO figures, private consumption expenditure rose by 7% during this time. This accelerated growth and well-being was possible because of, among other things, Modi government's visionary endeavour to increase employment of the masses. In 2014-2024, there has been a significant surge in employment with 17.9 crore more jobs been created and between 2017 and 2024 more than 4.7 crore youth in the age group 18-28 were brought to the fold of Employees' Provident Fund Organisation. This is a magical growth when compared to a meagre 2.9 crore increase in availability of jobs between 2004 and 2014.

These attainments are only a handful picked and prioritized here from a basket of numerous accomplishments that Mr Modi in 11 years of wise governance can claim. I know I'm doing disservice to one of the best Prime Ministers India was fortunate to have because lack of space will not allow me to enumerate the entire inventory, and I wish also to remain cautious lest the reader feels my praise fulsome in ways I don't want to sound.

6

Chronicling 11 Years of the Narendra Modi Government: Developmental Works, Policy Reforms, and Transformative Initiatives (2014–2025)

Dr. Hidam Ajit Meetei[1], **Bhavana Devi Tekcham**[2]

In the past eleven years, India has seen a remarkable change under **Prime Minister Narendra Modi's** leadership, characterised by inclusive growth, landmark policy reforms, bold governance, and a self-reliant vision that seeks to make India globally respected. This narrative highlights the key major developmental works, milestones, reforms, and initiatives that have characterised and changed the trajectory of India in the Modi era.

A Development-Centric Governance Philosophy

Since taking office, the Modi government has prioritised *"vikas"* or development, which has and since 2014 the focus of the government since 2014. The focus has been on welfare for all

1. Assistant Professor, Ancient History and Archaeology Department, Manipur University, 8014286951, hajitmeetei@gmail.com

2. Research Scholar, Ancient History and Archaeology Department, Manipur University, 9615317358, bhavanadevitekcham786@gmail.com

and sustainable growth in the long run. Accelerated and direct action to meet set ambitious targets is a sharp improvement and a break from the past, aiming for the benefits to reach every citizen. The core and the guiding philosophy that has shaped policy making and politics is *"development for all"*, which has shaped policy making from economic strategy to welfare schemes.

Digital India: Transforming the Delivery of Public Services

Digital transformation is a defining feature of this period in history. The Digital India initiative sought the creation of the necessary governance structures and provided digital services. The JAM Trinity of *Jan Dhan-Aadhaar-Mobile* deregulated welfare distribution, drastically shrinking leakages and ensuring the intended beneficiaries received direct benefit transfers (DBT), pensions, and subsidies without needing any intermediaries, facilitating graft-free governance and ensuring transparency.

The Aadhaar-enabled identification system provided the backbone for identification for various welfare schemes. The *Jan Dhan Yojana* also pioneered large-scale financial inclusion by adding over 500 million new bank accounts and bringing countless individuals into the formal sector.

Age of bold structural and economic alterations

Some of the changes that were brought forth in the pursuit of a resilient economic system include the following.

The introduction of the Goods and Services Tax (GST) is the most significant change in the country's taxation history. GST merged several indirect taxes and created a single market for the country. This also reduced the burden of compliance for many businesses.

The introduction of the Insolvency and Bankruptcy Code (IBC) brought in a new framework to manage bad loans and deal with distressed businesses.

The corporate tax cuts: India reduced its tax rate by half to increase domestic and foreign investments.

Easier business operations in India: Some steps were even aimed at deregulating the starting and operation of businesses in India, substantially improving India's global standing.

Make in India and Industrial Transformation

Make in India was launched in 2014 to foster manufacturing, foreign investment, and integrate India into the global economy. It sparked the domestic production of electronics, smartphones, and renewable energy projects. Policies are now geared toward "Made in India," enhancing industrial credibility while creating new jobs, significantly boosting manufacturing and exports.

Infrastructure Revolution: Roads, Railways, Airways, Urban India

A hallmark of progress has been the growth and expansion of the nation's infrastructure:

Roads & Highways: National highways saw a 60% increase. Bharatmala and Sagarmala projects significantly improved national connectivity and saw record highway construction.

Railways: India's next-generation, eco-friendly public transport innovation, Vande Bharat Express trains and modernisation of stations.

Act East Policy: Manipur became a gateway to Southeast Asia, with more emphasis on trade and cultural interchange across borders. The Integrated Check Post at Moreh, Manipur was built to make it easier to trade with Myanmar.

Urban Infrastructure: The Smart Cities Mission and Atal Mission for Rejuvenation and Urban Transformation (AMRUT) focused on drives to modernise urban centres.

Housing for All: Pradhan Mantri Awas Yojana (PMAY) focused on mass affordable housing for the economically weaker section by constructing millions of houses.

Empowerment through Social Welfare

Inclusivity remained a promise with these programmes. Reshape India's social landscape:

Ayushman Bharat: The largest government health insurance scheme in the world, offering coverage to 500 million+ insured.

PM Ujjwala Yojana: Has provided free LPG connections to more than 90 million economically disadvantaged families, enhancing the health and dignity of women.

PM Mudra Yojana: Provided Collateral-free microloans of over ₹ 32.4 lakh crore by 2025 with women beneficiaries at 68% and substantial benefit to SC, ST and OBC communities.

Lakhpati Didi and Drone Didi schemes: Helped rural women of India attain economic self-sufficiency and technological expertise.

PM Svanidhi: Specialised credit schemes for micro-entrepreneurial activities for street vendors.

Agricultural Reforms and Farmer Welfare

Transformative action for the rural heartland:

PM-Kisan Scheme: Direct income support to more than 110 million farmers.

Fasal Bima Yojana: Enhanced coverage for crop insurance.

E-NAM: Established an electronic national agriculture market.

Considerable increase in Minimum Support Prices (MSP) for crops.

Cultural Renaissance and National Security

The government promoted the construction of national icons and addressed a renewed cultural consciousness alongside bolstering security:

Restoration and construction of the Kashi Vishwanath Corridor and Ram Mandir in Ayodhya paved the way for integrating their historical relevance with modern identity.

Abolition of Article 370: The Special status of Jammu and Kashmir was revoked, fully integrating the region into the Union.

Surgical strikes and counter-terrorism action: Bold and decisive action against national security challenges the nation faces.

Environmental Leadership and Energy Security

India made significant strides in sustainability and renewable energy:

India assumes leadership in the International Solar Alliance, alongside the nation's ambitious solar and wind energy targets. The Clean Ganga Mission and Swachh Bharat Mission encompass the comprehensive challenges of sanitation, river rejuvenation, and waste management. India's biofuel advancements and the adoption of electromobility technologies in clean energy are a global benchmark.

Northeast and Borderlands: A New Development Agenda

The Northeast has witnessed unprecedented peace and integration alongside long-neglected innovation, connectivity, and new technology. The government sanctioned more than 3,600 projects amounting to ₹ 44,859 crore in the Northeast region, which included roads, airports, and logistics. The region received the development of ten new greenfield airports and the existing airport access in Manipur, which improved due to the UDAN scheme. Furthermore, Imphal's capital was connected to India's broad gauge railway network in 2023, which enhances

Manipur's integration with the nation. The signing of twelve peace accords has enhanced connectivity and investment and generated new regional prosperity and tranquillity.

Global Diplomacy and India's Resurgence

The international standing of the Modi government has raised India's global profile exponentially. India's G20 leadership, active international participation, and intense diaspora diplomacy have significantly enhanced the country's image as a confident, emerging power. The change in thought process, modulo governance, and ambition brought by Modi's government has ranged from policy and poverty alleviation to embracing financial inclusion. World-class infrastructure, alongside enabling technological leapfrogging, has been exceptional.

The legacy of bold reforms and keen visionary leadership, pursuing a developed and self-reliant India, was accomplished in the first term of Modi in 2014, and is the hallmark of the government's transformative actions. The Modi administration's eleven years have essentially transformed India's geopolitical thought, political structure, and national goals. The results were notable and holistic in nature, having resulted in improving poverty alleviation, enhancing financial services, developing infrastructure, and improving technology. The period starting from 2014 is now seen as characterized by bold policy changes, remarkable leadership, and most critically, the aim to make India a fully developed, self-reliant, and confident country.

References

11 years of development and prosperity in Northeast India. www.narendramodi.in. (n.d.). https://www.narendramodi.in/reader/11-years-of-development-and-prosperity-in-northeast-india

11 years of development and prosperity in Northeast India. www.narendramodi.in. (n.d.). https://www.narendramodi.in/reader/11-years-of-development-and-prosperity-in-northeast-india

11 years of modi govt A BEACON OF HOPE, good governance, development: Culture minister. Newsonair. (n.d.). https://www.newsonair.gov.in/11-years-of-modi-govt-a-beacon-of-hope-good-governance-development-culture-minister/

Arghya Sengupta, Jinaly Dani, Kevin James and Pranay Modi, Hamin Ast?: *A Biography of Article 370,* Navi Books, 2022, Chapter VI: 'Collapse', p. 72.

Governance track record | prime minister of India. (n.d.-a). https://www.pmindia.gov.in/en/governance-track-record/

How India's economy has fared under ten years of Narendra Modi. United Nations University. (n.d.). https://unu.edu/article/how-indias-economy-has-fared-under-ten-years-narendra-modi

India Today. (2024, March 17). *New laws, new tax regime: PM modi lists what's changed after 2014*. India Today. https://www.indiatoday.in/india/story/pm-modi-lists-changes-before-after-2014-new-laws-income-tax-ease-of-living-2515858-2024-03-17

Press Information Bureau. (n.d.-c). https://www.pib.gov.in/

Rahul Shibashankar. (2023). *Modi and India.* Vintage by Penguin Random House.

Pmindiaun. (n.d.-e). https://pmindiaun.gov.in/public_files/assets/pdf/75_Years_of_India.pdf

Press note details: Press Information Bureau. (n.d.-e). https://www.pib.gov.in/PressNoteDetails.aspx?id=154624&NoteId=154624&ModuleId=3

Press Information Bureau. (n.d.). https://static.pib.gov.in/

Press Information Bureau. (n.d.-d). https://www.pib.gov.in/EventDetail.aspx?ID=1210

Transforming India: Narendra Modi's 15 Day's bold initiatives in infrastructure and Welfare. (n.d.-f). https://organiser.org/2024/06/30/244923/bharat/transforming-india-narendra-modis-15-days-bold-initiatives-in-infrastructure-and-welfare/

7

Narendra Modi Ji: Architect of Forensic Transformation

Dr. J. M. Vyas[1]

India's remarkable journey under the leadership of Honourable Prime Minister Shri Narendra Modi Ji over the past eleven years has been shaped by his vision, resolve and commitment to justice. Among the many areas transformed during this period, forensic sciences hold a special significance, for they reflect his belief that justice must rest upon the firm foundation of science.

My association with Modi Ji began during his tenure as Chief Minister of Gujarat. In my very first meeting, I observed his awareness of the vital role forensic sciences play in governance. He believed that justice for even the weakest citizen required scientific methods of investigation. His conviction was clear: stronger scientific infrastructure ensures fairer, faster and more accurate justice. Guided by this belief, he transformed the Gujarat Forensic Science Laboratory into the Directorate of Forensic Science, equipped with modern technology. He personally supervised progress and ensured coordination between police services and forensic practices for the larger public good.

1. (Padma Shri Awardee) Vice Chancellor, National Forensic Sciences University.

His vision went far beyond Gujarat. Recognising the global shortage of trained experts, he envisaged the creation of the world's first dedicated university in this field. In 2009, the Gujarat Forensic Sciences University was established, and in 2020, under his stewardship as Prime Minister, it was elevated to the National Forensic Sciences University with the status of an Institute of National Importance. This historic step firmly positioned India as a leader in forensic education and research.

The growth of this institution has been remarkable. From five courses in 2009, the university today offers over seventy programmes with more than seven thousand students, including 300 international students across 14 campuses with the first ever Government overseas campus in Uganda. More than 37000 officers and professionals from 90 countries have been trained, and over 240 collaborations have been signed with national and global organisations. The university is also proud to host six state-of-the-art Centres of Excellence that drive cutting-edge research and innovation in specialised domains of forensic sciences. The Government of India has also designated NFSU as the nodal agency for a national programme worth 2000 crore rupees to strengthen forensic infrastructure in the country. This reflects Modi Ji's trust in the discipline and its potential to serve society.

A significant example of the national capacity built under his leadership came during the tragic Air India plane crash in Ahmedabad. Forensic experts were entrusted with the difficult responsibility of identifying the victims. DNA matching was undertaken on a war footing, and the work was completed with speed and precision, giving families the solace of certainty amidst grief. This demonstrated that forensic science, strengthened under his vision, has become indispensable in disaster response, justice delivery and national security. It showed the nation and the world that India could respond with both compassion and scientific rigour in the most testing circumstances.

For me, the journey has been more than five decades long as a forensic expert. Under his guidance, I have seen this discipline grow from a specialised laboratory service into a movement of global relevance. His knowledge, his relentless follow-up, and his foresight have always been a source of inspiration.

As the Vice Chancellor of NFSU, I remain deeply grateful for the guidance and trust bestowed upon me by Hon. Prime Minister Shri Narendra Modiji. His visionary leadership not only inspired the foundation of this university but also enabled my own transformation—from a forensic expert to an academician dedicated to nurturing future experts. NFSU stands as a living testimony to his belief that science must serve justice. On behalf of the institution, I reaffirm our unwavering commitment to contribute to his dream of Viksit Bharat 2047 through the advancement of forensic sciences in India and across the globe.

With profound respect and gratitude.

8

A Decade of Transformation: Transformative Governance under Prime Minister Narendra Modi: A Perspective on Educational Reforms and National Development

Prof. Javed Musarrat[1]

Abstract

Over the last eleven years (2014—2025), India has witnessed transformative changes under the leadership of Prime Minister Narendra Modi. This period has been characterised by landmark policy reforms, development strides, social welfare schemes, economic restructuring, and a visionary shift in the higher education ecosystem, collectively redefining India's global stature. From unprecedented infrastructure growth and digital transformation to the sweeping implementation of the National Education Policy (NEP) 2020, the Modi government has laid the foundation for a self-reliant, progressive, and knowledge-driven India. Notably, India's calibrated and confident handling of global trade issues, such as the recent tariffs imposed by the Trump administration, showcased the government's pragmatic economic diplomacy and strategic resolve. The country maintained firm negotiations while expanding trade partnerships with other global powers, a testament to Modi's

1. Vice Chancellor, Integral University, Lucknow

visionary global leadership. The article also includes reflections and institutional experiences from my tenure as Vice Chancellor at Baba Ghulam Shah Badshah University, Rajouri, J&K, and Integral University, Lucknow, UP, highlighting how visionary national policies were effectively implemented at the university level. With a firm focus on outcome-based education, raising Gross Enrollment Ratio (GER), and fostering global academic standards, the higher education sector stands as a powerful catalyst in the making of a 'Viksit Bharat' and 'Vishwaguru' India by 2047. This paper reflects on these developments with a particular emphasis on the National Education Policy (NEP) 2020, its implementation and the broader implications for realising the vision of Viksit Bharat@2047 and Vishva Guru, India as a Global Knowledge Leader.

Introduction

Prime Minister Narendra Modi's tenure, which began in 2014, has marked a significant departure from traditional governance approaches, ushering in a model that prioritizes inclusive development, digital transformation, policy-driven growth, and national pride. The government's vision has been to position India not merely as an economic power but as a global thought leader (Vishva Guru) by the time it completes 100 years of independence in 2047 (Viksit Bharat).

Infrastructure and Digital Transformation

The Modi government launched ambitious infrastructure programmes such as Bharatmala and Sagarmala, aimed at improving road and port connectivity. Under the UDAN scheme, regional air connectivity has expanded significantly, making air travel accessible to smaller towns (Ministry of Civil Aviation, 2024). The Smart Cities Mission has brought integrated urban planning and citizen-centric governance to over 100 cities (MoHUA, 2023). The Digital India campaign (2015) brought a paradigm shift in governance and service delivery. Digital payments witnessed exponential growth, with the Unified Payments Interface (UPI) becoming the world's largest real-time payment system (RBI, 2024). The integration of Aadhaar, Jan Dhan accounts, and mobile phones, famously referred to as the JAM Trinity, ensured effective Direct Benefit Transfer (DBT), eliminating middlemen and leakages in welfare schemes (Meity, 2023).

Social Welfare and Economic Empowerment

Flagship schemes such as Pradhan Mantri Awas Yojana (PMAY) provided over 3 crore houses to the urban and rural poor (MoRD, 2024), while Ujjwala Yojana brought clean LPG connections to more than 9 crore families (Ministry of Petroleum & Natural Gas, 2023). Ayushman Bharat, the world's largest publicly funded health insurance scheme, has covered over 50 crore individuals (National Health Authority, 2024).

On the economic front, initiatives like Startup India, Make in India, and the Production Linked Incentive (PLI) schemes have reenergized the manufacturing sector. India attracted over $749 billion in FDI during 2014 - 2025, reflecting investor confidence (DPIIT, 2025). The Goods and Services Tax (GST) reform unified the indirect tax system and broadened the tax base (MoF, 2024).

Education and NEP 2020: A Revolution in Learning

Among the most impactful reforms of the Modi government has been the formulation and implementation of the National Education Policy (NEP) 2020. This forward-looking policy seeks to create a holistic, flexible, multidisciplinary education system aligned with the needs of the 21st century. As Vice Chancellor of Integral University, it is heartening to mention the implementation of NEP 2020 in its true spirit. We restructured our academic offerings in line with Education 5.0/6.0, emphasized outcome-based education (OBE), encouraged interdisciplinary learning, and improved linkages with industry and research.

The Gross Enrolment Ratio (GER) in higher education rose from 23.7% in 2014-15 to 28.4% by 2022–23 (AISHE, 2023). National platforms such as DIKSHA, SWAYAM, and NAD have expanded access to quality learning, especially in remote areas. Skill development programmes under Skill India have trained over 1.5 crore youth in emerging areas such as artificial intelligence, robotics, and data science (NSDC, 2024).

India on the Global Stage

India's rising global influence under Prime Minister Modi is equally remarkable. The hosting of the G20 Presidency in 2023 signified India's strategic diplomatic maturity. India has assumed leadership in climate action through the International Solar Alliance and voiced the concerns of the Global South in multilateral forums. Defense exports surged from ₹ 1,940 crore in 2014 to over ₹ 23,000 crore in 2024 (Ministry of Defence, 2025), and India's pharmaceutical sector emerged as the "Pharmacy of the World" during the COVID-19 pandemic. Recently, when faced with tariff impositions by the Trump administration on Indian exports, the Modi government responded with calibrated countermeasures and diplomatic engagement, securing concessions while reinforcing India's sovereign trade interests. These developments underscore India's transformation from a reactive participant to a proactive leader on the global stage.

My Reflections and Institutional Contributions as Vice Chancellor

Having had the privilege of serving as the Vice Chancellor of both Baba Ghulam Shah Badshah University, Rajouri, J & K from (2015-2020) and Integral University, Lucknow (2021-2025), during the tenure of Prime Minister Narendra Modi's transformative leadership, I have personally witnessed and contributed to the sweeping changes envisioned under his government, particularly in higher education. At Baba Ghulam Shah Badshah University, nestled in the picturesque but historically underserved district of Rajouri, Jammu & Kashmir, we harnessed the central government's thrust on digital and educational infrastructure to bridge regional disparities. Initiatives such as the expansion of digital classrooms, student scholarship facilitation through the National Scholarship Portal, and the integration of skill-based programmes into the mainstream curriculum allowed us to align with national goals while catering to local needs. During this period, the university's outreach extended to marginalised communities, truly embodying the Prime Minister's vision of 'Sabka Saath, Sabka Vikas.'

At Integral University, Lucknow, the adoption of NEP 2020 has been more of a mission than a mandate. We undertook a comprehensive institutional transformation, overhauling curricula, introducing multidisciplinary and choice-based learning models, promoting faculty development, and emphasizing employability and innovation, transforming Integral University from a Teaching & Research University into a Research-Intensive University. Further, the Research and development were integrated with real world applications, and we successfully aligned academic projects with the goals of Atmanirbhar Bharat. We also prioritized internationalisation and industry partnerships to prepare our students for global competitiveness. These experiences reaffirm our belief that the Modi government's education reforms are not only well-intentioned but also powerfully actionable when supported by visionary institutional leadership. As a stakeholder in this national journey, I remain deeply inspired by the call to build a Viksit Bharat and reclaim our position as a Vishva Guru. The last eleven years have been a period of not only change but purpose-driven evolution, and I am proud that my journey as an academic leader has paralleled this national renaissance.

Vision for the Future: Viksit Bharat and Vishva Guru

The foundational reforms undertaken in the last eleven years have laid the groundwork for India's future as Viksit Bharat, a developed, inclusive, and knowledge- driven nation by 2047. Prime Minister Modi's statesmanship is anchored in seva (service), sankalp (resolve), and vikas (development). As an academic leader, I see India not only gaining economic and geopolitical stature but also emerging as a source of moral, philosophical, and intellectual leadership globally, a Vishva Guru in the truest sense.

Conclusion

The eleven years of the Modi government represent more than a policy cycle; they symbolise a national awakening. From rural connectivity to digital leadership, from educational transformation to diplomatic assertion, India under Prime Minister Modi has charted a bold, confident course. As we move toward the centenary of our independence, the path laid out promises not only material prosperity but also a civilisational renaissance. With continued commitment, India is poised to inspire the world with its blend of tradition, technology, and transformative governance.

References

1. All India Survey on Higher Education (AISHE). (2023). Ministry of Education, Government of India.
2. Ministry of Education (2020). National Education Policy 2020.
3. Ministry of Civil Aviation (2024). Annual Report on UDAN Scheme.
4. Ministry of Housing and Urban Affairs (MoHUA). (2023). Smart Cities Mission Progress Report.
5. Reserve Bank of India (2024). Digital Payments Report.
6. Ministry of Electronics and IT (Meity). (2023). JAM Trinity and DBT Evaluation.

7. Ministry of Petroleum & Natural Gas (2023). PM Ujjwala Yojana Dashboard.
8. National Health Authority (2024). Ayushman Bharat Statistics.
9. Department for Promotion of Industry and Internal Trade (DPIIT). (2025). FDI Inflows Dashboard.
10. Ministry of Finance (2024). GST Annual Review.
11. National Skill Development Corporation (NSDC). (2024). Skill India Mission Report.
12. Ministry of Defence (2025). Annual Defence Export Data.

9

Beyond growth, crafting a healthy, knowledge driven self reliant Bharat

Dr. Jayanthi V

Introduction

As Vice Chancellor of Sapthagiri NPS University and a healthcare professional, I have observed the 11-year journey of the Narendra Modi government with a sense of admiration and inspiration. This Gandhi Jayanti 2025 release provides not just an opportunity to reflect, but also to celebrate how policies in health, education, social welfare, innovation, and economy have come together to shape a healthier, smarter, and more confident India.

For me, two sectors stand out—**healthcare and education**—because they are deeply interlinked. A healthy citizen learns better, and an educated citizen makes healthier choices. When combined with a forward-looking economic and social framework, these two pillars become the foundation of nation-building. Over the past decade, India has taken major strides in these areas, laying the path for a *Viksit Bharat* by 2047.

Education: A Renaissance in Learning

The **National Education Policy (NEP) 2020** is perhaps the most transformative step in Indian education in decades. By prioritizing holistic growth, creativity, flexibility, and technology integration, it has reshaped how students learn. At Sapthagiri NPS University, I've seen its impact directly—our engineering and medical programs now foster collaboration across disciplines, encouraging skill-based and innovative learning.

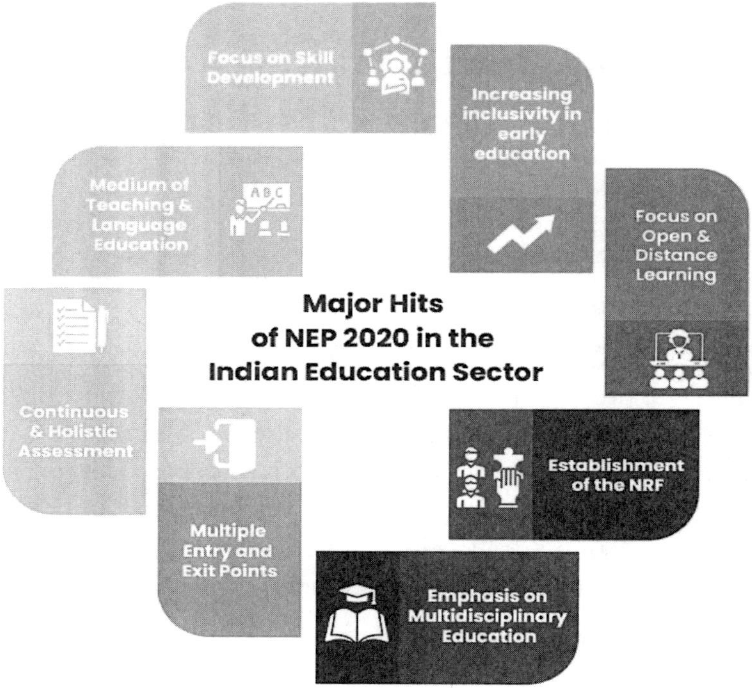

The government has also expanded inclusivity, raising reservations for persons with disabilities from 3% to 5% and mandating support for their education. In healthcare, landmark legislations such as the **National Medical Commission Act (2019)**, **Medical Termination of Pregnancy Act (2021)**, **Assisted Reproduction Act** (2021), and **Surrogacy Act** (2021) have modernized regulation, ethics, and protections. Similarly, the **National Commission for Allied and Healthcare Professions Act** (2021) standardized 56 allied health courses, creating a stronger workforce.

Aligned with the **Skill India Mission**, which has trained over 2.27 crore youth with an investment of ₹2 lakh crore, these reforms are fueling biomedical innovation, AI research, and low-cost healthcare technologies. Our students, too, have developed affordable biomedical prototypes inspired by this environment.

Higher education capacity has grown with new IITs in Tirupati, Jammu, Dharwad, and Palakkad, and expansions at National Skill Training Institutes across cities. These moves created thousands of new seats and faculty positions.

But what truly stands out is the human touch initiatives like **Pariksha Pe Charcha**, where the Prime Minister directly engages with students. I recall streaming this at our university; the calm reassurance in his words visibly eased student anxieties. This blend of large-scale reform and personal connection has given Indian education a new identity—ambitious, empathetic, and future-ready.

Healthcare: From Access to Assurance

The government's healthcare reforms reflect a people-first approach. The **Ayushman Bharat – Pradhan Mantri Jan Arogya Yojana (PM-JAY)**, launched in 2018, remains the world's largest government-funded health insurance scheme, covering **50 crore citizens**. Over **36 crore health cards** have been issued, saving families an estimated **₹ 1.25 lakh crore** in healthcare costs.

In 2024, the government expanded its commitment to senior citizens through **Ayushman Vaya Vandana**, offering coverage to all above 70 years of age, regardless of income. Already, over 58 lakh elderly citizens have received treatments worth nearly ₹ 500 crore. Importantly, **ASHA and Anganwadi workers**—the backbone of India's public health system—are also covered, honoring their service.

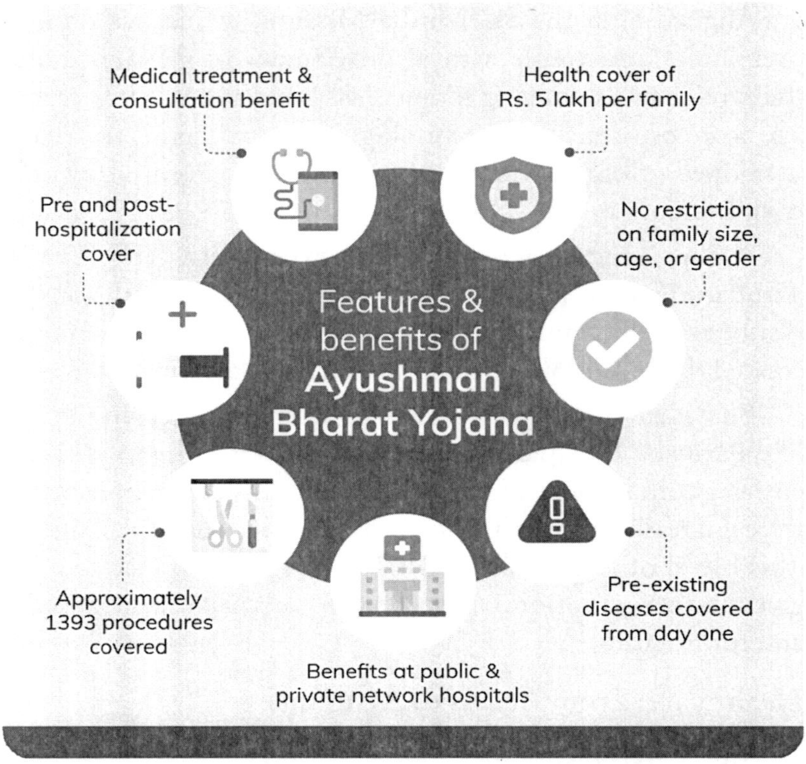

Key features of Ayushman Bharat Yojana: coverage, access, and benefits

The **Ayushman Bharat Digital Mission (ABDM)** is creating a national digital health backbone. With 78 crore health IDs and 55 crore linked health records, people now have secure, portable access to their medical history. The **e-Sanjeevani telemedicine platform** has enabled more than 36 crore consultations, making it the largest of its kind globally. Meanwhile, over 10,000 **Jan Aushadhi Kendras** now supply affordable generic medicines at up to 90% lower prices, and primary care is being strengthened through thousands of health and wellness centers.

Medical education has also seen historic growth. The number of colleges has nearly doubled from 387 to 780, and **AIIMS institutions** have risen from 7 to 23. MBBS seats more than doubled to 1.15 lakh, and PG seats crossed 79,000. For students at Sapthagiri and across India, these reforms mean not just better training but also wider opportunities to serve in both rural and urban communities.

India's COVID-19 response showcased resilience and leadership. With 220 crore vaccines administered and millions shared globally under **Vaccine Maitri**, India emerged as a trusted health partner. Preventive programs like **Mission Indradhanush** accelerated immunization, while maternal health was strengthened through the **Pradhan Mantri Matru Vandana Yojana**, now extended to cover the second girl child—supporting both mothers and gender equity.

This transformation is about more than numbers—it reflects **trust, accessibility, and impact**. Maternal mortality has declined, life-saving medicines are within reach, and confidence in India's public health system is stronger than ever.

Social Welfare: Building Dignity from the Ground Up

Development must begin with dignity, and over the last 11 years, social welfare programs have redefined quality of life in India:

- **Swachh Bharat Mission**: Over **12 crore toilets built**, eradicating open defecation and improving health.
- **Har Ghar Jal: 14 crore households** connected with clean drinking water.
- **Ujjwala Yojana**: Over **10 crore families** transitioned to LPG, replacing hazardous firewood. **PM Garib Kalyan Anna Yojana**: Provided free food grains to **81 crore citizens**, ensuring food security.

- **PM Jan Dhan Yojana:** With **53 crore bank accounts opened**, the foundation for digital banking and direct benefit transfers was created.

Har Ghar Jal in action: Households now have tap water under the Jal Jeevan Mission

These schemes have improved attendance in schools, reduced disease, and enhanced women's safety—creating a ripple effect on education and healthcare.

Women and Children: Empowering Generations

The **Beti Bachao, Beti Padhao** campaign has altered mindsets by stressing that a daughter's education is as valuable as a son's. The government has further strengthened women's representation with reservation in politics, ensuring that voices of women shape policy at every level.

Women's empowerment is also economic. From smokeless kitchens under Ujjwala Yojana to digital banking access through Jan Dhan accounts, women are better positioned to lead households and careers.

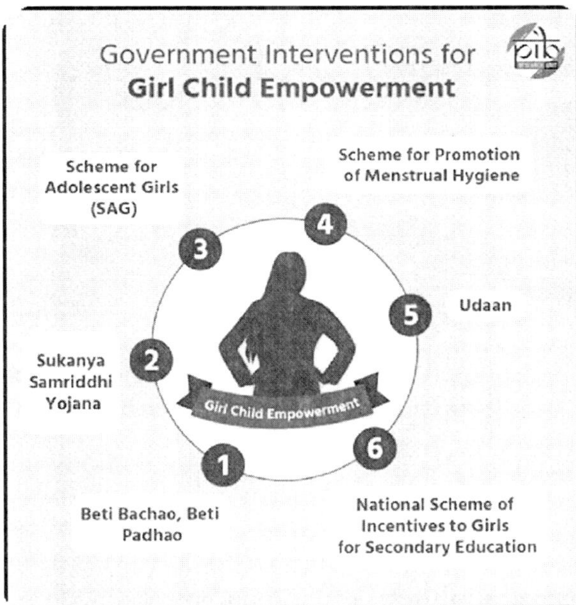

Nutritional programs such as **Mission Poshan 2.0** and **Saksham Anganwadi** target malnutrition among children and mothers. The **POSHAN Tracker** uses technology for real- time monitoring. Combined with **PMMVY**, which offers maternity benefits and encourages positive attitudes toward girls, these initiatives ensure healthier families and stronger communities. "Swasth Nair, Sashakt Parivar Abhiyaan" in covergence with "Poshan Maah" will start from 17th September 2025 culminating on Gandhi Jayanth, has been launched by the government.

Economic Growth and Self-Reliance

In 2004, India was the **11th largest economy**; by 2014, it had not advanced further. Over the past 11 years, however, innovative policies have propelled India to become the **Fourth-largest economy** with GDP growth averaging 7.4%.

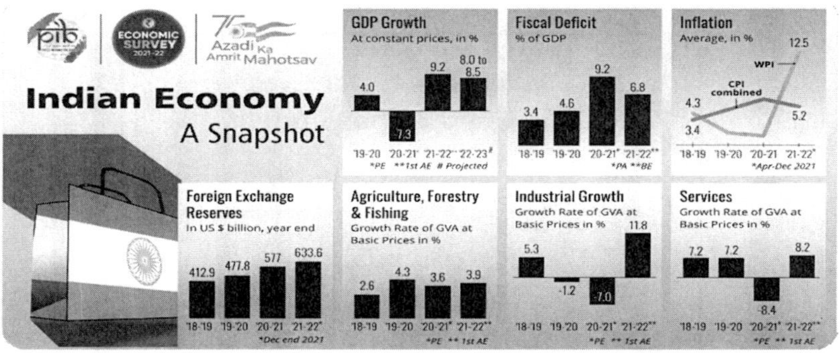

India's climb in global economic rankings: emerging as a leading economy

The **Atmanirbhar Bharat Abhiyan** has been central to this transformation. By encouraging MSMEs, boosting FDI, and promoting *Vocal for Local*, India has become the **second-largest producer of mobile phones,** manufacturing over **33 crore units annually.** In 2025, India overtook China to become the top smartphone exporter to the U.S.—a milestone under the *Make for the World* vision.

Reforms in the MSME sector, removal of angel tax for startups, and government-backed challenges like the **Toycathon** and **App Innovation Challenge** have nurtured indigenous innovation. Self-reliance in fertilizers, solar manufacturing, and electric vehicles further demonstrates strategic foresight.

Innovation, Startups, and Research

India's innovation ecosystem has exploded in scale.

With **1.61 lakh startups recognized** and India ranked **third globally in unicorn count**, entrepreneurship has become the heartbeat of youth aspirations. Investments of over **₹ 2 lakh crore** in skill development have built a workforce ready for industries of the future.

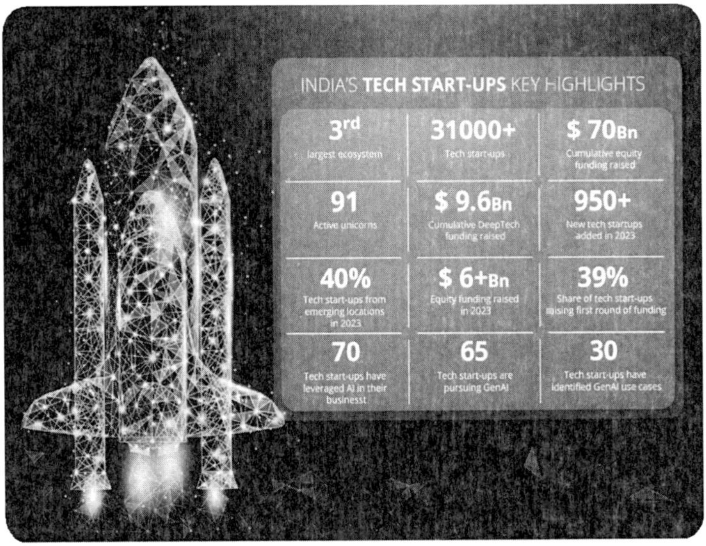

India's booming tech startup ecosystem: scale, unicorns, and innovation in 2024.

Policies like the **BioE3 Policy** and **Vigyan Dhara Scheme** integrate biotechnology, environment, and economy, encouraging high-performance biomanufacturing. Initiatives in electric vehicles and green energy ensure that India's growth is not only rapid but sustainable.

Sports: From Playgrounds to Podiums

Sports have been embraced as a tool for national unity and global pride. Programs like **Khelo India** and **Target Olympic Podium Scheme** (**TOPS**) have professionalized talent development. Over **2,700 athletes.**

A proud moment: Khelo India athlete on the podium at National Games 2025

we have been nurtured under these schemes, with significant results:

- **7 medals at the Tokyo Olympics (2021).**
- **6 medals at the Paris Olympics (2024).**
- **29 medals at the Paris Paralympics (2024)**—India's best-ever tally.
- **124 medals at the 2022 Asian Games** won by Khelo India athletes.

These achievements highlight how grassroots programs have turned India into a serious sporting nation.

Digital India: The Technological Backbone

The **Digital India Mission** has connected **1.3 billion citizens** to affordable internet, transforming healthcare, education, banking, and governance.

- **Online learning** through DIKSHA, SWAYAM, and PM e-Vidya has democratized education.

- **Telemedicine** and **virtual diagnostics** have become integral to healthcare training.
- **Digital banking** through Jan Dhan and UPI has made India the global leader in real-time payments.

The success of platforms like CoWIN and Aarogya Setu during COVID-19 proved India's ability to use digital tools for mass-scale governance.

Governance, Unity, and Nation-Building

Whether it is **Unified Pension Scheme** offering security to government employees, or the **Khelo India movement** nurturing athletes, or even environmental strategies through **solar energy and EV policies**, the unifying theme is clear: governance as service.

This philosophy—from *Pradhan Mantri* to *Pradhan Sevak*—has shaped an inclusive, people- first model of leadership.

Conclusion

The last 11 years have been about **healing minds and educating hearts.** Healthcare has become accessible, education has become innovative, women have been empowered, and the economy has been revitalized. India today is not just building infrastructure; it is nurturing human potential.

As an educator, I see classrooms filled with curiosity and confidence. As a healthcare professional, I see hospitals better equipped and patients better served. As a citizen, I see a nation rising with self-belief and compassion.

This decade reminds us that true progress is measured not only in economic rankings but in healthier families, empowered women, confident youth, and innovative minds. With **wellness and wisdom** as its guiding principles, India is on course to realize the dream of a *Viksit Bharat* by 2047.

10

Viksit Bharat @ 2047 *via* Education

Prof. K. K. Aggarwal[1]

More than a decade ago, a young girl asked the then President Dr. A.P.J. Abdul Kalam as to when will India become developed and his positive response at that time was the first indication for giving credibility to our hope of becoming a developed country. However, a goal without a roadmap and any fixed timeline is rather hypothetical, howsoever good it may be.

It was left to the vision of our beloved Prime Minister Shri Narendra Modi to define a timeline by fixing the goal of *Viksit Bharat @ 2047*. Our visionary Prime Minister was fully conscious that setting a goal even with a timeline will have no meaning unless a complete roadmap is drawn. It was in this context that he dedicated a full 25 year period from 2022 to 2047 as *Amrit kaal* during which our great country Bharat is to ensure that it has become from *Vikassheel to Viksit*. The Prime Minister had a very clear vision that all this will require a multi-prong approach encompassing all dimensions. He set up a clear objective for the size of economy, need for upgradation of infrastructure (whether physical or digital) and ensured that we become a self-dependent country in all aspects to the extent possible. He very consciously adopted the terminology of *Atmanirbhar Bharat* as he was more than clear that without

1. President, South Asian University, New Delhi

being self-reliant there is no possibility of becoming *Viksit* and unless we can provide vision to the whole world we shall certainly not be able to achieve the destined goal of our dear Bharat becoming *Vishwaguru.*

As is clear from several narratives in his speeches, Prime Minister Modi is having no doubt in believing that only our strengths can make us great. He also is very conscious of the fact that every country has to have its own uniquely determined path for overall growth and development. No country in the world has ever gone to the top position by emulating others. I am reminded of a saying by one of my school teachers, who used to say that probably one can sometimes pass the examination by copying, but no one can secure the highest rank by copying. Our beloved Prime Minister is a practitioner with a clear goal of high rank in the entire world.

In the light of all this, Prime Minister Modi brought to the focus that education can be the only medium for the real transformation and that too when our education system and policy is India-centric. I see it not as a coincidence but a God inspired design that before dedicating the education policy to the Nation (after its approval from the cabinet), the foundation stone for Ram Mandir was laid in Ayodhya. I, as an academic see it as a clear heavenly signal that our education policy will be drawing its strength from our culture, our heritage, our value system or put in proper words our *sanskars* and our *sanskriti.*

Our National Education Policy (NEP-2020) is a document which has evolved after the highest possible consultation in the entire world on any policy matter. Also, to the best of my knowledge no head of the nation has spent so much time on any single policy as our visionary Prime Minister has done while discussing all aspects of Education Policy.

The need of the hour, as has been reiterated by the Hon'ble Prime Minister is that it is necessary to have its faithful and genuine implementation by all concerned. He has repeatedly reiterated that this policy is not to be treated as a mere document but has to be embodied as the spirit of the nation and has to be imbibed as such. For the first time in the history of the country, we have a policy which takes care of pre-primary education and continues up to post-doctoral research. For the first time, the Prime Minister has indicated that the aim of our education is to produce competent global citizens, which are routed in Bharatiya Sanskriti, whether they work in Bharat or outside Bharat. For the first time, the policy is aiming to balance life and livelihood. The convergence of knowledge and skills for all courses at all levels is the hallmark of this policy.

The graduates from the Universities who equip themselves with this policy in the real sense will have the greatest autonomy not only for the University administration, but also to each and every student of the University. All this is possible only with the due empowerment of the teachers and therefore the Prime Minister has laid very special emphasis on Teacher Education. He has repeatedly stated that there are several attributes which can be developed only in the early childhood such as value system, respect to the society, to the family and to the nation. There has been a misconceived notion that our Bhartiya Sanskriti doesn't fit into the modern education. He has asserted that it is the other way round and expressed that our culture leads to modern education, which still has miles to go. Many like me agree *cent percent*.

Producing Problem Solvers as against rote learners is the aim of this Policy. Sensitivity towards Ethics, Resource Optimisation, Sustainability, Environment, Empathy, Outcome driven, Creative and Innovative nature are the parameters which he has asserted more often than anyone else. He has also laid great emphasis on research *(anusandhan)*. He believes that PhD is only the beginning of Catalytic academic leadership in this complex world. He has ensured the shift from our youth going abroad to Foreign Universities coming here.

History of the country will remember Prime Minister Modi as the grassroot education reformer for the overall transformation of the country.

11

Brief Contribution to Society: PM Modi Government

Prof. (Dr.) K P Yadav[1]

Serving the poor and the marginalised has been the underlying promise of the government, a promise that is guided by the principle of 'Antyodaya' which means that the goal of development isn't complete till that it reaches the last human in our society. The Indian Constitution says that every citizen as equal, and guarantees a life of dignity for each of them. Yet despite several decades since independence, many citizens continued to lack the basics to lead a life with dignity and honour. This should be changed, and change needs rapidly without break. Since 2014, the government led by Hon'ble Prime Minister Narendra Modi has been committed to a model of development that ensures that no one should left behind.

Development that guarantees basic facilities such as drinking water, electricity, healthcare, toilets, Gas cylinders, Basic and higher education, and financial inclusion to all, which not just to a select few names. In the last 11 years, the Modi government has launched and implemented many welfare schemes and social justice efforts to empower its own people. The results of such irreversible empowerment can be seen in programmes i.e. MUDRA Yojana and Stand Up India, which are creating a large pool of young entrepreneurs from marginalised groups

1. VC, Mats University, Raipur, CG.

and weaker section of the society. More than half of the 45+ crores loans given under MUDRA have been given to interested reserve category entrepreneurs. This is ushering empowerment of not just individuals, but is also a means to empower the neglected societies. In line with its welfare programme, the Modi government's historic decision to provide reservations for economically weaker sections provided much-needed support to poor households and thereof.

As part of its vision of inclusive development, the government has undertaken many solutions and ways to empower Divyangjan, Transgender persons, De-notified and Nomadic tribes, and other such hitherto unserved or underserved people. The government's resolve for social justice was evident in its decision to implement OBC and EWS reservations in all India quota seats in medical education, ensuring that students from these groups can also aspire to become doctors in affordable government Institutions. Under the Namaste scheme, the government aims to eradicate unsafe sewer and septic tank cleaning practices/methodologies, so that sanitation workers can live with their dignity.

An integral element of PM Modi's government has been making to recognize icons of social empowerment. To commemorate the sacrifices of tribal fighters for the country, the government has declared November 15 of every year, Bhagwan Birsa Munda's Jayanti as Janjatiya Gaurav Divas (Tribal Honor Day). This kind of recognition builds pride among communities by highlighting their efforts to nation-making. The government's efforts to extend welfare provisioning and poverty alleviation have received recognition from global institutions. The Modi government efforts removed extreme poverty in the country. The Global Multidimensional Poverty Index released by the United Nations Development Programme and the Oxford Poverty and Human Development Initiative has also credited India with a reduction in all ten of its Multidimensional Poverty Indicators.

12

Reforms and Revolutions in the Higher Education Institutions of India

Prof. (Dr.) K. Prathapan[1]

Over the last eleven years (2014–2025) under Prime Minister Shri. Narendra Modi, India's higher education landscape has undergone substantial reforms and transformations at the policy level, along with structural revolutions. These changes aim to modernise Higher Education Institutions (HEIs), improve global competitiveness, enhance access and equity, and align with the demands of a knowledge-driven economy of the world.

A detailed overview of the key policy-level developments and revolutions in HEIs during this period are listed below:

1. National Education Policy (NEP) 2020 – A Landmark Reform of the century

   Policy Level reforms:

   First major overhaul of the education system in 34 years of the Independent India.

   Aims for holistic, multidisciplinary, skill based education and flexible curricula.

1. Vice-Chancellor, D. Y. Patil Agriculture & Technical University, Talsande

With major emphasis on skill development, critical, creative thinking, and research.

Key Features:

Multidisciplinary institutions: Goal to make all HEIs multidisciplinary by 2040.

Multiple Entry and Multiple Exit options with an Academic Bank of Credits (ABC).

Undergraduate education restructured to 4 years with flexible options of honours and degree.

One umbrella common Higher Education Commission of India (HECI) proposed to replace UGC and AICTE.

Emphasis on regional languages, online education, courses on online platform and digital universities.

2. Institutional Restructuring and Accreditation

Major Revolutionary Steps:

Push towards autonomy: More institutions are given graded autonomy.

Institutions of Eminence (IoE): Launched to create world-class universities (IISc, IITs, private universities).

National Institutional Ranking Framework (NIRF): Encouraged quality benchmarking and competition.

Revamping of NAAC accreditation system to outcome-based metrics.

3. Governance and Funding Mechanism Reforms

Changes Introduced:

Funding shifted toward performance-based mechanisms.

Establishment of Higher Education Financing Agency (HEFA) to fund infrastructure and R&D.

Increased private sector participation in HEIs.

Introduction of single regulatory body (HECI) (yet to be fully implemented).

4. Focus on Research and Innovation

   Reforms:

   National Research Foundation (NRF) proposed to fund research equitably across disciplines.

   Promoting start-up ecosystems and incubation centers in HEIs.

   Programmes like PM Research Fellowship (PMRF) and SPARK.

5. Technology-Driven Transformation

   Digital Revolution in HEIs:

   SWAYAM: Free online courses for HEI learners.

   SWAYAM PRABHA: 32 DTH channels for education.

   National Digital Library, DIKSHA, and e-PG Padashala expanded.

   Post-COVID, rapid digitization of teaching-learning via online mode/blended learning.

6. Internationalization and Global Outreach

   Steps Taken:

   Policy support for foreign universities to set up campuses in India.

   Guidelines for twining programmes, student exchange, and credit transfer with international universities.

   Launch of Study in India initiative to attract foreign students.

7. Emphasis on Skill Development and Employability

   Initiatives:

   Integration of vocational education into higher education (NSQF alignment).

Push for industry-academia linkages.

Expansion of community colleges and skill-based degree programmes.

8. Social Inclusion and Gender Equity

   Progressive Policies:

   Scholarships and support for SC/ST/OBC and women students.

   Establishment of Gender Champion Cells, Divyangjan-friendly campuses.

   Focus on rural and tribal education access through digital and satellite modes.

9. Emphasis on Indian Knowledge Systems (IKS)

   Promoting courses on Indian languages, culture, philosophy, and traditional sciences.

   Establishment of Indian Knowledge Systems division under the Ministry of Education.

10. Regulatory simplification and Governance Modernisation

    One-nation one-data platform efforts (e.g., AISHE database revamp).

    Push for transparency, outcome-based education, and NEP-aligned governance models.

Conclusion

The Modi government's era has seen a revolutionary shift from regulation to facilitation in higher education, marked by the NEP 2020 as a cornerstone reform. These reforms target inclusivity, flexibility, global alignment, and innovation-led growth.

13

11 Years of Transformative Leadership: The Making of a Self-Reliant India Amid Global Turbulence

Dr. K Satyanarayan Reddy

Introduction

In the annals of modern Indian history, few epochs have witnessed as profound a transformation as the 11-year tenure (2014–2025) of Prime Minister Narendra Modi's government. This era will be remembered not just for the scale of progress but for the spirit with which the nation navigated global turbulence and decisively marched towards Atmanirbharta: self-reliance. As the world grappled with political uncertainty, economic upheavals, pandemics, and shifting power dynamics, India found within itself a wellspring of resilience, innovation, and hope.

This is the story of a New India; rooted in tradition, driven by technology, and propelled by the faith and determination of 1.4 billion citizens.

The Spirit of Inclusive Governance

When the Modi government assumed office in 2014, it inherited a country of great promise but daunting challenges: persistent poverty, crumbling infrastructure, fractured social trust, and sluggish job creation. The new leadership's vision was clear: "Sabka Saath, Sabka Vikas, Sabka Vishwas, Sabka Prayas"; Together, for everyone's growth and trust, with everyone's effort.

The scale of inclusive outreach over 11 years is staggering: 81 crore (810 million) people have received free food grains under the PM Garib Kalyan Anna Yojana; 15 crore rural households have tap water for the first time; over 12 crore toilets under Swachh Bharat Mission have transformed health, hygiene, and dignity for women and children. The Ujjwala Yojana revolutionised kitchens for 10 crore families, while the world's largest health assurance scheme, Ayushman Bharat, shields over 50 crore Indians.

Financial empowerment became a national movement. Over 52 crore loans under PM Mudra Yojana provided wings to small entrepreneurs. The Jan Dhan-Aadhaar-Mobile (JAM) trinity enabled direct benefits and plugged leakages, while ensuring bright economic prospects for even the remotest citizen.

Building a New Social Fabric

India's empowerment story is incomplete without acknowledging its most marginalised. In a historic move for gender justice, the government expanded paid maternity leave from 12 to 26 weeks. Mudra's collateral-free loans reached women entrepreneurs at scale, and special schemes supported pregnant and lactating mothers. Social justice also moved to the centre stage, with a majority of ministers from Scheduled Castes, Tribes, and OBCs, reflecting the country's true diversity.

The transformation goes beyond numbers. It is visible in the aspirations of millions of girls going to school, families accessing quality healthcare, and women entrepreneurs leading rural enterprises. It is seen in the reduction of multidimensional poverty; a staggering 25 crore people have escaped the clutches of deprivation since 2014, as highlighted by the NITI Aayog's report on poverty reduction.

Revitalising Education and the Youth

"India's greatest asset is its youth," PM Modi has observed time and again. The last 11 years have witnessed a paradigm shift in how India educates, skills, and inspires its young citizens. The National Education Policy (NEP) 2020, the first in over three decades, promotes a flexible, skill-driven, and value-based curriculum geared towards the demands of a digital and dynamic world.

Over 1.6 crore youth have gained employable skills under the Pradhan Mantri Kaushal Vikas Yojana. India's global research footprint is growing, with new IITs and IIMs, world-class universities, and over 1.6 lakh recognised startups providing employment and solutions across sectors. The PM SHRI scheme is modernising 14,500 schools, bringing best-in-class facilities to every corner. India now stands as the world's third-largest startup ecosystem, a symbol of how government policy and youth aspiration can together chart new vistas.

Robust Infrastructure: Connecting Dreams

Transformation in India's infrastructure is evident and widely lauded. From highways and high-speed trains to digital highways and new airports, every mode has seen quantum leaps in capacity, quality, and reach. The Atal Mission for Rejuvenation and Urban Transformation (AMRUT) and Smart Cities Mission are shaping vibrant, future-ready cities. The UDAN scheme is democratizing air travel, taking the first flight from small towns to India's metro airports.

Digital India is now a global success story. Affordable high-speed internet (with a 97% fall in data cost), nearly universal 5G coverage, and digital public infrastructures such as UPI and Aadhaar have changed how Indians pay, learn, do business, and even access government services. No other nation has replicated digital inclusion on such a scale.

New Growth Engines: Make in India, Start-Up India, and Beyond

India's journey to self-reliance took firm root with flagship programmes such as Make in India, Start- Up India, and Digital India. "Vocal for Local" became a clarion call not only for consumers but for companies and policies, ensuring Indian talent met global standards in manufacturing, pharmaceuticals, electronics, and defence.

"Make in India" turned the country into a major global manufacturing hub, boosting exports and creating jobs. Defence manufacturing, electronics, and critical API pharmaceuticals saw significant growth, reducing import dependence and building economic resilience. The improved "Ease of Doing Business" index ranking (from 142 in 2014 to 63 in 2019) signals a friendlier investment environment.

Agricultural Renaissance: From Annadata to Entrepreneurs

Agriculture, the backbone of rural India, received renewed policy focus. The PM-Kisan Samman Nidhi infused direct support to over 11 crore farming families, with more transparent, timely, and comprehensive coverage than ever before. Schemes for irrigation (Pradhan Mantri Krishi Sinchai Yojana), market reforms (e-NAM), and crop diversification bolster farm incomes and resilience; crucial in a global environment riddled with supply shocks and food insecurity.

The government's support for agri-tech startups, food processing industries, and robust warehousing ensures that farmers are not just cultivators but also entrepreneurs and value creators. The Ministry of Jal Shakti, created in 2019, underscores the nation's determination to tackle water scarcity with new urgency.

Healthcare for All: Protection in Uncertain Times

Ayushman Bharat, the world's largest health assurance scheme, offers protection to over 50 crore people. Its success is emblematic of India's priorities: affordable, accessible, and high-quality care for all. The COVID-19 pandemic was a trial by fire, but it was also a testament to India's adaptability and scientific prowess. From ramping up PPE and ventilator production to executing the world's fastest vaccination drive, India emerged as a global model for crisis response.

The establishment of AIIMS in every state, a vast network of medical colleges, and digital health platforms underscore a new health infrastructure fit for the challenges of the 21st century.

The Green Commitment: Sustainability at the Core

In a world rocked by climate change, India stands out for its ambitious climate goals and innovative green initiatives. Under PM Modi's leadership, India crossed the installed renewable energy capacity of 175 GW and pledged to reach 500 GW by 2030. The International Solar Alliance, championed by India, now comprises over 120 countries uniting for solar energy proliferation. National movements like Swachh Bharat and the Clean Ganga Mission have combined technology, policy, and people's participation for unprecedented results.

"Our lifestyle is our message," the Prime Minister has asserted, linking India's civilisational ethos to its environmental actions; from turning LED usage into a mass movement to championing "LiFE" (Lifestyle for Environment) as a global campaign.

Global Standing: India as a Responsible Power

In a turbulent world with wars, shifting alliances, and economic crises, India has emerged as an anchor of stability and a voice for the Global South. At forums like the G20,

Quad, BRICS, and SCO, India advocates for inclusive growth, climate justice, and reformed multilateralism. Vaccine Maitri, the programme to supply COVID-19 vaccines to over 100 countries, showcased India's humanitarian leadership.

India's firm diplomatic stance, especially evident in recent developments vis-à-vis major powers, demonstrates a confident, self-assured nation that seeks collaboration but asserts its interests fearlessly.

Recent Developments: Operation Sindoor and Trade Policy Assertiveness Operation Sindoor: Defending the Nation's Honour

In 2025, as India faced renewed threats from across its western border, Operation Sindoor was launched against Pakistani incursions and terror activities. The operation combined the might of advanced technology, precise intelligence, and ground forces, earning admiration for its swift execution and minimal collateral damage. This resolute action sent an unambiguous message: India's sovereignty and the safety of its citizens are sacrosanct.

International observers noted India's strategy: balancing firmness with caution, pre-empting threats without crossing international norms. Operation Sindoor is now seen as a textbook example of calibrated response, boosting public morale and underlining India's zero tolerance for terror.

Taking a Stand Against the U.S. Tariff Policy

The global economic landscape has been shaken by rising protectionism and new tariff barriers, notably by the United States on Indian goods. Instead of yielding, the Modi government took a forceful stand, initiating reciprocal tariffs, launching diplomatic outreach, and using the WTO platform to assert the principles of fairness and mutual benefit. India's approach was pragmatic; open to negotiation but firm on sovereignty and the interests of its producers.

This response signals a maturing foreign policy, where engagement and self-interest are balanced. Such actions have increased India's credibility as a trading partner and as a nation that defends its rights, fostering pride and confidence at home.

Rising Through Crisis: Lessons from the Global Pandemic

The COVID-19 pandemic tested even the strongest nations. Yet, India's response, producing vaccines at scale, providing essentials to millions, leveraging technology for lockdown management, stands tall. "Jaan bhi, Jahan bhi" (Life as well as Livelihood) was not just a slogan but an entire approach to pandemic management: protect lives, sustain livelihoods.

When the world turned inward, India turned outward, exporting vaccines, medicines, and technology even in the toughest situations, cementing its role as the "pharmacy of the world."

Innovation and Digital Leap

India is now a beacon for digital innovation. The UPI payment system has transformed transactions, bringing even the smallest street vendor into the digital ecosystem. Aadhar, with over a billion enrollments, enables efficient and targeted delivery of benefits. Initiatives like Cowin for universal vaccination, National Digital Health Mission, and promotion of Artificial Intelligence in governance mark India's arrival as a digital powerhouse.

Startups, from fintech to agritech, space to health, have blossomed under this government's investor- and talent-friendly regimes, driving economic inclusion and grassroots innovation.

Empowerment, Participation, and 'Minimum Government, Maximum Governance'

Turning away from the red tape of yesteryears, PM Modi's mantra, 'Minimum Government, Maximum Governance' has reimagined how policy is created and services delivered. Technology- enabled platforms, DBT (Direct Benefit Transfer), faceless tax systems, and digital documentation have drastically cut corruption and leakages, putting people at the centre.

The Aspirational Districts Programme is a shining example: targeting the "last mile" with data-driven, decentralised interventions, it is transforming backward regions into engines of growth.

Security and Internal Stability

India's internal security situation has seen marked improvement. From the abrogation of Article 370, bringing greater integration and development to Jammu & Kashmir, to successful containment of Left-Wing Extremism, the Modi era has focused on bridging divides: physical, economic, and psychological. Border infrastructure now matches the best globally, and emergent digital tools aid in pre-empting and countering threats.

Reflections and the Road Ahead

As we step into the next decade, India stands at a cusp: young, ambitious, often messy, but brimming with hope and potential. The 11 years of Modi government have charted a new course, towards dignity for the poorest, opportunity for all, and pride in our identity.

Atmanirbhar Bharat; Self-Reliant India is not just about manufacturing but about mindsets: trusting local talent, celebrating Indian innovations, building resilient supply chains, and forging partnerships on India's terms. Despite global headwinds, trade wars, health crises, and conflicts; India's stature as a trusted partner, responsible regional power, and beacon of democracy has grown manifold.

As generations look back, the legacy of this era will be shaped not just by statistics or reports but by stories: of a girl from a remote village aspiring to become an astronaut, a farmer using a smartphone to check global prices, a scientist innovating for the world, and an entrepreneur building a digital empire from her home.

The 11 years of the Modi government stand as a testament to what is possible when vision, commitment, and public participation align. India's march from poverty to possibility, from dependency to self-reliance, is a beacon for a fractured world searching for hope and stability.

Let this journey inspire not just Indians, but all nations; that through unity, courage, and the right leadership, destinies can be changed. The dream is alive, the resolve is firm, and the best, truly, is yet to come.

Major References:

(1) **Official Government Releases and Annual Reports:**

(a) VIKSIT BHARAT KA AMRIT KAAL: SEVA, SUSHASAN (Compilation of 11 years)

(b) Governance Track Record – Prime Minister of India

(c) Know the PM – Prime Minister of India Profile

(d) 11 Years of Transformative Governance Highlights

(2) **Notable Media Coverage and Analysis:**

(a) "11 big achievements in 11 years of PM Modi government," Times of India

(b) Invest India – "8 Years of Modi Government: 8 Major Achievements"

(c) Wikipedia – "Premiership of Narendra Modi" (for timelines, statistics, reforms)

14

ले. जनरल के.टी. पारनाईक
पीवीएसएम, यूवाईएसएम, वाईएसएम (से.नि.)
राज्यपाल, अरुणाचल प्रदेश

सत्यमेव जयते

राजभवन
ईटानगर - 791111

"एक भारत श्रेष्ठ भारत"

भारत अविश्वनीय विविधताओं एवं सांस्कृतिक रूप से समृद्ध देश है, जो अपनी समृद्ध सास्कृतिक विरासत अनेक भाषाओं, विविध व्यजनों और जीवंत परंपराओं के लिए जाना जाता है। सांस्कृतिक विकास के समृद्ध इतिहास से इसकी पहचान है। सांस्कृतिक विरासत इसकी सबसे बड़ी संपत्तियों में से एक है। भारत में कला, संगीत, नृत्य और साहित्य बेशुमार है, प्रत्येक क्षेत्र राष्ट्रीय ताने-बाने में अपना अनूठा स्वाद जोड़ता है। अपने विशाल मतभेदों के बावजूद भारत विविधता में एकता के सिद्धांत को मूर्त रूप देते हुए एकजुट है। एक भारत, जो भारत की अवधारणा इस एकता का जश्न मनाती है और एक ऐसे राष्ट्र की कल्पना करती है जो अपनी विविधता का इस्तेमाल अद्वितीय महानता प्राप्त करने के लिए करता है।

प्रौद्योगिकी के इस युग में, जिसने भौगोलिक सीमाओं को सीमित कर दिया है, विभिन्न क्षेत्रों के लोगों के बीच कला एवं सांस्कृतिक आदान-प्रदान से राज्यों एवं देशों के मध्य बेहतर तालमेल और सद्भावना को बढ़ाने की पहल करते हुए, जन-कल्याण चिंतक, सर्वसमावेशी दृष्ट्रिकोण रखने वाले भारत के **माननीय प्रधान मंत्री, श्री नरेन्द्र मोदी जी** ने **सरदार वल्लभभाई पटेल की जयंती, 31 अक्टूबर 2015 को एकता दिवस** पर **"एक भारत श्रेष्ठ भारत"** की परिकल्पना की थी। यह अभियान भारत की सांस्कृतिक जीवंतता का जश्न मनाने के लिए शुरू की गई थी, साथ ही हमारे देश के नागरिकों में राष्ट्रवाद और सांस्कृतिक जागरूकता पैदा करने के लिए एक मजबूत तंत्र स्थापित किया गया था।

"एक भारत श्रेष्ठ भारत" पहल एक एकीकृत और सांस्कृतिक रूप से एकीकृत भारत के निर्माण की दिशा में एक महत्वपूर्ण कदम है। राज्यों और केंद्र शासित प्रदेशों को सांस्कृतिक आदान-प्रदान और आपसी शिक्षा के लिए प्रोत्साहित करके, यह न केवल राष्ट्र की एकता को मज़बूत करता है, बल्कि प्रत्येक भारतीयों की सांस्कृतिक चेतना को भी समृद्ध करता है। इसके तहत भारत की विविधता को समझने और साझा पहचान की भावना को बढ़ावा देने के लिए राज्यों की समृद्ध विरासत और संस्कृति, रीति-रिवाजों और परंपराओं को प्रदर्शित करना है।

"एक भारत श्रेष्ठ भारत" का राष्ट्रीय एकता और अखंडता को बढ़ावा देने में गहरा प्रभाव पड़ा है। भारत के विविध क्षेत्रीय सांस्कृतिक ताने-बाने आपस में एक साथ मिलकर, एक मज़बूत और समृद्ध राष्ट्र के निर्माण में सहायक हैं। यह राष्ट्रीय गौरव की भावना को बढ़ावा देता है, अंतर्राज्यीय सद्भाव को प्रोत्साहित करता है, और यह सुनिश्चित करता है कि युवा पीढ़ी भारत के विशाल सांस्कृतिक धरोहर को सुरक्षित एवं संरक्षित करेंगे। यह पहल लोगों को, लोगों से जोड रही है जो वास्तव में भारत में लोगों के बीच एकता, शांति और सद्भावना को बढ़ावा दे रही है।

"एक भारत श्रेष्ठ भारत" के तहत अपनी आबादी के विविध कौशल और प्रतिभाओं का लाभ उठाकर, भारत को वैश्विक आर्थिक महाशक्ति बनाने तथा **"मेक इन इंडिया"** और **"डिजिटल इंडिया"** जैसी पहलों से नवाचार एवं उद्यमशीलता को बढ़ावा देकर रोजगार पैदा किया जा रहा है और अर्थव्यवस्था को बढ़ावा दिया जा रहा है। एक संयुक्त भारत, समान आर्थिक लक्ष्यों की दिशा में काम करते हुए उल्लेखनीय प्रगति और समृद्धि प्राप्त कर रहा है।

"एक भारत श्रेष्ठ भारत" एक एकजुट, समृद्ध और सामंजस्यपूर्ण राष्ट्र का दृष्टिकोण है, जिसके तहत हम अपनी विविधता को अपनाकर, सामाजिक सद्भाव को बढ़ावा तथा आर्थिक विकास को गति देकर, प्रौद्योगिकी में आगे बढ़कर और सतत विकास पर ध्यान केंद्रित करके, भारत को अद्वितीय महानता प्राप्त करा सकते हैं। एकता और समावेशिता के सिद्धांतों द्वारा निर्देशित प्रत्येक भारतीय का सामूहिक प्रयास एक उज्जवल और अधिक समृद्ध भविष्य का मार्ग प्रशस्त करेगा। हम सब मिलकर भारत को न केवल एक बल्कि दुनिया में सर्वश्रेष्ठ बना सकते हैं। जैसे-जैसे यह पहल आगे बढ़ेगी, यह पूरे भारत में सद्भावना और एकजुटता के एक मज़बूत बंधन के साथ **"एक भारत श्रेष्ठ भारत" - एक भारत, महान भारत** बनने की दिशा में कामयाब होगी।

पारनाइक

लेफ्टिनेंट जनरल के.टी. पारनाईक

पी.वी.एस.एम., यू.वाई.एस.एम., वाई.एस.एम.(से.नि.)

15

Eleven Years Of Modi, As I Experienced It

Lt. Gen. (Dr.) Konsam Himalay Singh, Retd

When Shri Narendra Modi became the Prime Minister of India in 2014, I was serving in Jammu and Kashmir in a very responsible military assignment. Speculations were agog with varied ideas as to how long Sri Modi would last as the PM of the country, given the meteoric rise of a "Chaiwallah". From senior politicians, seasoned bureaucrats, civil society groups and from Manipur (the state from which I come) to Jammu to Kanya Kumari, people at large were not very sure as to how the destiny of the country would be under the leadership of Shri Modi in those tumultuous times.

Sooner than later, it slowly and steadily revealed that our country was seeing another Sardar Vallabh Bhai Patel like leadership after 60 years or so. We began to see the combined qualities of many iconic figures of India in one man who was determined to deliver India, that is Bharat, a place under the sun yet again in the comity of nations in the 21 century. He began to consolidate and revive the values and the pride of Indian civilisation which was lost many centuries ago. The civilisational pride of India, which once expanded to the entire Asian mass and beyond began to slowly unfold in our eyes in the contemporary world. The idea and practice of Yoga, the practice of ancient Vasudev Kutumbhakam, and many other Indian Philosophy and science spread far and wide to suit a modern world, which was yearning for spiritual gap. That India under Sri Modi has begun to deliver the answer to many of the threats to the very existence of mankind on this planet is a given. The leadership provided by India in the global south or even during the covid pandemic speaks for the yeomen stride India has made.

While lifting hundreds of millions of poor Indians out of poverty, many more are on their way to enjoying the social and economic status and respect within and outside the country due to social and economic revolution taking place in the last ten years. Indians abroad are no longer shy of being called "Indians". That to my mind is a huge contribution of Sri Modi. The nation is now proud of saying' "Bharat mata Ki Jai".

Securing the nation from threats from within and without have been another big achievement. The strategy of removing any terrorists threat to our people and the country wherever they may be is a paradigm shift in our approach as seen during "OP SINDOOR". The "ATMA NIRBHAR" policy particularly in the field of defence related production is a huge step in the right direction to secure our country. The multiple terrorists groups in the North East India, in Kashmir and in the hinterland are beginning to realise the futility of playing proxies to outside forces.

Yet, we are still miles away from achieving Modi's dream of Vikshit Bharat. We surely are on the correct path to achieve the same by 2047 subject to dealing with multiple dimensions of governance. From achieving equitable progress at grassroots, infrastructure, sustained 7% economic growth, political stability, education and health need further push in the years to come. I pray to the God almighty that our nation truly achieve our aim by 2047.

16

Views, Experiences, and Key Initiatives Undertaken During the 11 Years of the Modi Government

Er. Kordor Lamare[1]

The views, experiences and key initiatives undertaken during the 11 years of the Modi government are as follows:

1. **Views:-** Shri Narendra Modi has outlined his Vision for the India of tomorrow which resonates with the BJP's philosophy of "Sab Ka Saath, Sab Ka Vikas". Economic policies of Modi's government focused on privatisation and liberalisation of the economy, based on a neoliberal framework. Modi liberalised India's foreign direct investment policies, allowing more foreign investment in several industries, including in defence and the railways. Prime Minister Narendra Modi's strategic vision that has placed self-reliance, innovation, and indigenous development at the centre of national policy. The Government's Goal is for India to be a USD 4.0 trillion economy when we celebrate the Platinum Jubilee of our Independence. Moreover, the

1. Er. Kordor Lamare, Executive Engineer (WR), Department of Water Resources

Prime Minister has given his clarion call for establishing a New India by 2022. Create 100 million additional jobs in the manufacturing sector by 2022. Increase in the manufacturing sector's share in the GDP to 25% by 2022. Creating required skill sets among the urban poor and the rural migrants to foster inclusive growth. Viksit Bharat 2047 is the government's vision to drive the mission of making India a completely developed nation by its 100th anniversary of Independence in 2047. The vision is based on four pillars: Yuva (Youth), Garib (Poor), Mahilayen (Women), and Anna data (Farmers). Foreign policy of the Modi government, also referred to as the Modi doctrine is associated with the policy initiatives made towards other states by the current government of India after Narendra Modi assumed the office of prime minister on May 26, 2014.

2. **Experience:-** India becomes the fastest growing large economy in the world under the NDA Government. It has been a historic year for the Indian Economy. The first eight years of Modi's premiership, India's GDP grew at an average rate of 5.5% compared to the rate of 7.03% under the previous government. He is the first sitting Prime Minister since Indira Gandhi in 1971 to return to power with a full majority. Narendra Modi is the only Prime Minister, apart from late Jawaharlal Nehru, to win three consecutive elections as leader of a political party in India. Respectfully dedicated to all those who have offered continuous sacrifices for the unity and integrity of society.

3. **Key initiative:-** Pradhan Mantri Jan Dhan Yojana (PMJDY) • Pradhan Mantri Suraksha Bima Yojana (PMSBY) • Pradhan Mantri Jeevan Jyoti Bima Yojana (PMJJBY) • Atal Pension Yojana (APY). Pradhan Mantri Jan Dhan Yojana is the main key initiative

of Modi Government. PMINDIA • Make in India • Swachh Bharat Abhiyan • NITI Aayog: Transforming India's Development Agenda • Campaign aims to achieve the vision of a 'Clean India' by 2nd October 2019. The Swachh Bharat Abhiyan is the most significant cleanliness campaign by the Government of India. Make in India – Initiatives. For the first time, the sectors of railways, insurance, defence, and medical devices have been opened up for more Foreign Direct Investment (FDI). The maximum limit in FDI in the defence sector under the automatic route has been raised from 49% to 74%. The first eight years of Modi's premiership, India's GDP grew at an average rate of 5.5% compared to the rate of 7.03% under the previous government. Pradhan Mantri Nai Manzil Scheme Yojana, Pradhan Mantri LPG Subsidy PAHAL Yojana (DBTL) Modi Sagar Mala Yojana, Pradhan Mantri Suraksha Bandhan Yojana. PM Surya Ghar: Mufti Bijli Yojana is a government scheme that aims to provide free electricity to households in India. The scheme was launched by Prime Minister Narendra Modi on February 15, 2024. Under the scheme, households will be provided with a subsidy to install solar panels on their roofs. The 4 pillars of Make in India initiative are New Mindset, New Sectors, New Infrastructure, and New Processes. A few of the most noteworthy schemes launched in 2025 are PMJDY (Pradhan Mantri Jan Dhan Yojana), PMJJBY (Pradhan Mantri Jeevan Jyoti Bima Yojana), and PMSBY (Pradhan Mantri Suraksha Bima Yojana). PM-JAY provides cover of ₹ 5 lakhs per family per year for secondary and tertiary care hospitalisation to over 10.74 crore poor and vulnerable families (approximately 50 crore beneficiaries). There is no cap on the family size under the scheme. As on February 2018, Pradhan

Mantri Jeevan Jyoti Beema Yojana (PMJJBY) has benefitted 5.22 crore families with a life insurance cover of ₹ 2 lakh on payment of a premium of only ₹ 436/- per annum per subscriber. India First aims to create a landscape brimming with resources, support, and streamlined regulations for tech startups. It envisions India as a global leader in tech solutions, exporting groundbreaking ideas and fostering a robust network of innovative minds. **The best examples of initiatives in the work environment** (i) Offering to help when no one asks, (ii) Resolving minor problems before they become serious, (iii) Taking on a task that others have avoided, (iv) Enquiring about what a job entails, (v) Providing career advice and support to colleagues, (vi) Seeking career advancement opportunities. Since it was created in 2015, NITI Aayog has neither been able to offer fresh thinking on the economy nor has it functioned as a mediator between the center and the states. A federal institution facilitating political-level cooperation is crucial to respond to the demands of a modern economy as on 6 Feb 2025. The Government of India has approved the PM Surya Ghar: Muft Bijli Yojana on 29th February, 2024 to increase the share of solar rooftop capacity and empower residential households to generate their own electricity. The scheme has an outlay of Rs 75,021 crore and is to be implemented till FY 2026-27, 2 Jun 2025.

Modi Government brought India to higher level for the country as a whole. He is dynamic leader who showed every important thought for the Nation.

Thanking You

17

Revolutionising Higher Education through Institution Building and Skill Development during 2014-2025

Dr. Krishnan Chalil[1]

Basing on the endogenous growth model, the social and economic policies of India during the last eleven years were driven by tremendous emphasis on education and health. The social sector has been given paramount importance in the development agenda. In this sector, education is the pivotal spectrum which is the basis of the overall development of any country. Understanding this fact, the Modi Government in the last eleven years has consciously intervened in the field of education, especially, in higher education. The release of the National Education Policy 2020 and its implementation across the country is the revolutionary development during this period. As mandated by the NEP 2020, several initiatives like Academic Bank of Credit, multiple entry and exit, four year and five year integrated UG programmes, internationalisation of higher education, strengthening of National Testing Agency, National Credit framework, transformation of Higher

1. Professor and Head, Department of Economic Studies and Policy Central University of South Bihar, Gaya, Email:drckcalicut@gmail.com

Education Financing Agency, India Skill Mission, etc., are meticulously implemented. Efforts in the direction of achieving 50 per cent GER in higher education by 2035, many other strategic decisions have also been crafted. Many new HEIs have been established during this period which has resulted in more enrolment as well as quality of education. During the period 2014-25, seven new IITs, 16 IIITs, 3,000 ITIs, 390 universities, 15 AIIMS and seven IIMs, have been added. The number of medical colleges increased from 387 in 2014 to 780 in 2025, witnessing an increase of 130%. Similarly, the number of medical PG seats also increased from 31185 to 74306 (138%) during the same period. Another landmark in the field of higher education is sharp increase in the number of Indian HEIs appearing in the QS World Ranking. Its number has increased from 11 in 2015 to 46 in 2025. This development has been possible through the committed actions of the government through different schemes like Institutions of Eminence, Anusandhan National Research Foundation, One Nation One Subscription etc. Access and equity are the two major issues in Indian higher education which could be solved in a major way through the PM student Loan Portal (Vidya Lakshmi Portal). Prime Minister, Sri. Narendra Modi reiterated that "Skill development and employment are crucial needs in India. Our government is consistently working in this direction." In this connection, the PM Internship Scheme announced in the Union Budget 2024-25 is a remarkable initiative launched by the Indian government, which aims to bridge the gap between academic learning and real-world experience by offering internships across the top 500 companies.

Despite the appreciable progress in the march towards an equitable, affordable and accessible higher education, many of the ideals mentioned in the NEP 2020 is yet to be realised. To mention a few of them: the establishment of the National Research Foundation, Higher Education Commission of India, measures to curb commercialisation of education etc. Similarly, considering the critical importance of research, the research and innovation investment in India is, at the current time, only 0.69% of GDP as compared to 2.8% in the United States of America, 4.3% in Israel and 4.2% in South Korea. We hope that the rest of the years, the present government would concentrate on these grey areas.

18

11 Years of Transformative Governance: A Needonomics Analysis of the Modi Era

Prof. (Dr.) Madan Mohan Goel[1]

Over the past eleven years, India has witnessed a significant transformation under the leadership of Prime Minister Narendra Modi. His government has undertaken a wide range of policy reforms, developmental initiatives, and governance innovations that have redefined India's trajectory in both domestic and global spheres.

Needonomics School of Thought (NST) takes upon itself the responsibility to chronicle, analyze, and interpret these transformations with clarity, objectivity, and depth. Our aim is to provide an authentic, well-researched, and analytical account of the government's performance — offering insights for scholars and the general public. This initiative aligns with NST's core values: understanding economics through the lens of needs over greed, human dignity, and ethical progress.

A Decade Plus One: Redefining India's Growth Story

The Modi government's journey since 2014 is marked by initiatives that seek to make India self-reliant (Atmanirbhar

1. Proponent Needonomics & Former Vice Chancellor

Bharat), digitally empowered, economically inclusive, and socially equitable. These include bold decisions and long-term policy shifts in the areas of infrastructure, economy, governance, social welfare, foreign policy, and national security. NST's analysis covers the following thematic areas:

1. **Economic Reforms with Ethical Foundations**

   Modinomics has aimed to simplify, formalise, and digitize the Indian economy. Landmark reforms like GST, Insolvency and Bankruptcy Code (IBC), Digital India, Jan Dhan Yojana, and Startup India are not just economic interventions — they reflect a shift from entitlement to empowerment. NST views these as steps towards building a need-based economy that rewards productivity and innovation, while reducing corruption and leakage.

2. **Social Welfare and Direct Benefit Transfers**

   The Modi government has expanded the welfare state with a focus on targeted delivery. Schemes like Ujjwala Yojana, Ayushman Bharat, PM Kisan, and Har Ghar Jal aim to reach the last person in the queue. NST appreciates the elimination of middlemen through technology-driven governance, thus reflecting the core principle of *doing more with less*.

3. **Infrastructure for New India**

   From rural roads to urban metros, from smart cities to digital highways, the infrastructure push has been monumental. The PM Gati Shakti Master Plan, Bharatmala, and UDAN aviation scheme are shaping the physical and digital future of India. These investments represent productive use of public expenditure — a hallmark of need-based economics.

4. **Cultural Confidence and Governance Ethics**

   India's soft power has been strategically revived —

through International Yoga Day, promotion of Indian languages and traditions, and positioning India as a Vishwa Guru. NST recognizes this as a move toward ethical nationalism, fostering self-respect and cultural pride without arrogance.

5. **Foreign Policy: Assertive and Balanced**

   India's diplomatic posture under Modi has evolved into a proactive, pragmatic, and principled approach. From Neighbourhood First to Act East, Vaccine Maitri to the G20 Presidency, India has emerged as a global consensus builder. NST interprets this as diplomacy rooted in needs of peace, development, and mutual respect.

6. **Digital Governance and Inclusion**

   Digital India has not only empowered citizens with access and efficiency but also democratized information and services. Portals like DigiLocker, UMANG, and CoWIN exemplify governance that is transparent, inclusive, and accountable — aligning with NST's ethos of value-based administration.

7. **Challenges and Constructive Critique**

   While achievements are many, challenges remain — including unemployment, climate concerns, federal tensions, and institutional accountability. NST believes that critical evaluation without cynicism is vital. The focus should remain on reforms with results, not just rhetoric.

NST's Role: Research, Reflect, Recommend

Needonomics School of Thought (NST) undertakes this responsibility not to praise blindly or criticize unfairly, but to document with diligence, analyze with academic integrity, and recommend with responsibility. Our approach is rooted in Indian ethos, inspired by Gita-based action without attachment, and guided by the principle: *"Produce according to need, not greed."* We aim to publish detailed thematic reports, public lectures, and policy briefs to contribute meaningfully to India's developmental discourse. The stakeholders of the economy are expected to be street SMART (simple, moral, action-oriented, responsive and transparent) in playing their role.

Conclusion

Eleven years of Modi-led governance present a compelling case for study — not just in political terms but in socio-economic and ethical dimensions. The NST initiative seeks to uncover the truths behind the numbers, the spirit behind the slogans, and the impact beyond the intentions. This is more than a review — it is a tribute to the idea of India progressing through purpose, performance, and people-centric policy.

19

National Education Policy 2020: Transforming India's Human Resource

Prof. Manabendra Dutta Choudhury[1], Dr. Dhanawantari L. Singha[1]

Abstract

The National Education Policy (NEP) 2020 is a turning point in India's education system introduced by the Government of India under the leadership of Prime Minister Narendra Modi with the vision to make India a global knowledge leader. The objective behind the launch is to address the significant needs of the 21st century with the advanchment of technology that replaces the earlier NEP 1986 and its 1992 revision. The significant needs are the rapid globalisation, technological advanchment in education, and the rising demand for skill-based, inclusive, and multidisciplinary education. In this chapter, we present the foundation of NEP 2020, highlighting the need of its formulation, discusses the its key features, including its focus on holistic and flexible learning, the 5+3+3+4 curricular structure, Early Childhood Care and Education (ECCE), promotion of regional languages, vocational education, research promotion through the National Research Foundation, and digital learning integration. Moreover, special attention is given to the various challenges faced in implementation of the system such as funding constraints or uneven funding opportunities, teacher preparedness, infrastructure gaps, and resistance to systemic changes

1. Rabindranath Thakur Vishwavidyalaya, Hojai, 782435, Assam, India, Corresponding author email id: drmdc@bioinfoaus.ac.in

from traditional structure. In conclusion, the chapter presents a overall view of NEP 2020, emphasizing its potential to reshape Indian education and the hurdles that must be addressed for its effective realisation.

Keywords: National Education Policy 2020 (NEP 2020); Holistic and Multidisciplinary Learning; Skill-based Education; Equity and Inclusion; Implementation Challenges.

1. Brief background on the formulation of NEP 2020

The National Education Policy 2020 was approved on 29th July 2020 by the Union Cabinet chaired by the Prime Minister Shri Narendra Modi, with former Cabinet Secretary T. S. R. Subramanian, switching the 34 years old 1986 education policy and becoming the major education policy of 21st century (PIB, Mumbai 2020). The initiation for drafting the NEP guidelines started in 2019 under the leadership of Dr Krishnaswamy Kasturirangan, former Indian Space Research Organisation (ISRO) Chief. The policy was approved in 2020, but launched the process of drafting in 2015 by the Government of India, under the leadership of Prime Minister Narendra Modi as a part of "Transforming India" initiative. The policy emphasizes foundational literacy, skill development, research, digital learning, and value-based education, while integrating Indian knowledge traditions with global best practices. With the vision of making India a global knowledge superpower, NEP 2020 aims to ensure quality, equity, and inclusion in education at all levels. One of the major reason for the vision of NEP 2020 came from the Goal 4 of Sustainable Development Goal 4 (SDG4) under the global education development agenda adopted by India in 2015 that seeks to "ensure inclusive and equitable quality education and promote lifelong learning opportunities for all" by 2030 (NEP 2020, MHRD, Govt. of India).

2. Earlier education policies before NEP 2020

In India, earlier, two major education policies were there

before 2020. The first education policies was the National Policy on Education (NPE) (1968). This policy mainly emphasized on equal educational opportunities and compulsory education up to age 14 for all. The second policy was the National Policy on Education (NPE) (1986, revised 1992). This policy mainly focused on restructuring higher education, vocational training, and women's education.

3. The need for an updated education policy after NEP 1986 and its revision in 1992

The demand for new education policy arisen due to the requirements of skill-based education, huge development in technology, and globalisation by the 21st century. This has led to the requirement of a more flexible, multidisciplinary, and holistic education system (Figure 1).

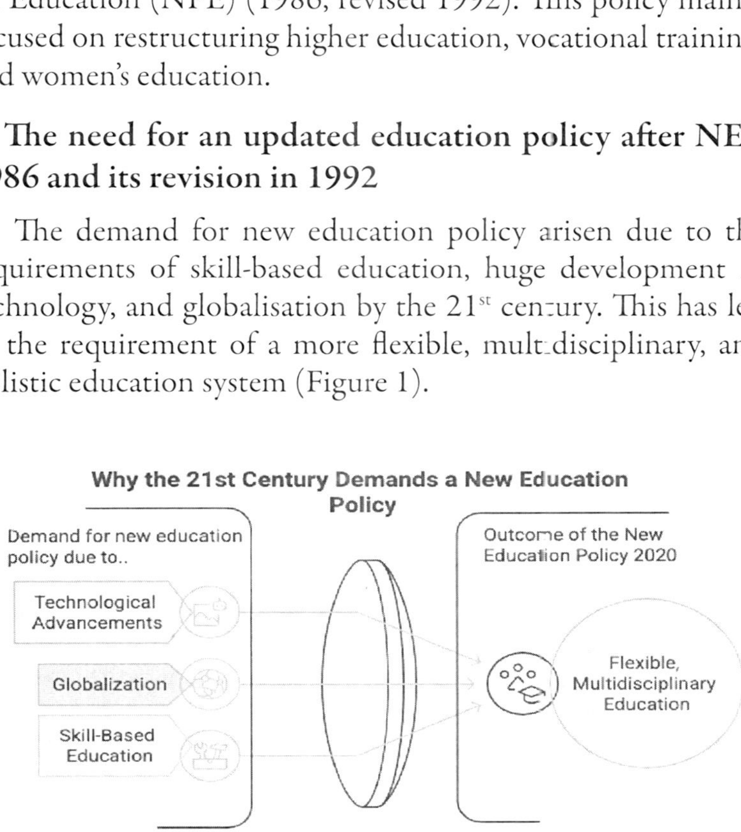

The image was prepared using Napkin AI

Figure 1: The reason for demanding a new education policy by the 21st century is the technological advanchments, globalisation of education and skill-based education for a flexible and multidisciplinary education with more practical learning aproaches.

The reasons that led to the requirement of New Education Policy can be explained with

(a) Technological Advancements

The groundbreaking progress in technological advancements have been achieved specially in the field of Information and Communication Technology (ICT) in the 21st century (Yeamin, 2019). To meet the technological advanchments in ICT such as with the rise of digital tools for e-learning, application of big data and AI in education, India need the technological integration in school and higher education. The application of technological advanchments will improve the traditional pedagogical methods and the ability of the students learning. Further, in connection to it, NEP 2020 emphasise on the development of National Education Technology Forum for exchanging communication and guiding how to use the technological advanchments in higher education. Furthermore, India is continously progressing in the area of science, economy, social science and countries leadership. The refore application of such technological advanchments in education system is not only essential but necessary.

(b) Globalisation and Competitiveness

Globalisation has renovated education by creating an interconnected world where students are no longer competing only within their local or national boundaries but on a global stage. This shift demands the development of graduates who are not only academically sound but also globally competent. In this context, education must focus on equipping learners with international exposure, the ability to think critically, creatively, and innovatively, and the skills to adapt to diverse cultural and professional environments (Herlinawati et al., 2024). Cross-cultural understanding, communication, and collaboration have become essential attributes for success in a highly competitive global workforce (Erfan, 2024). Therefore, the education system must prepare students to meet international standards, adapt to rapid technological advancements, and contribute meaningfully to the global knowledge economy.

(c) **Skill-based and Vocational Education**

Earlier education policies in India primarily focused on theoretical knowledge and academic excellence with mostly lectures and periods which are monotonous, with limited emphasis on practical skill development or vocational training (Tilak et al., 2003; Kingdon et al., 2007). Syllabus was mostly constructed for theory only with less scope for practical applications. However, with the changing socio-economic landscape and the rise of diverse industries, there emerged a growing need for an education system with practical applications and hands on skill beased training (UNESCO, 2012). The older policies, including NEP 1986 and its 1992 revision, fell short in addressing this gap, leaving many graduates underprepared for employment. Therefore, a restructured approach through skill-based and vocational education became essential to empower students with employability skills, promote innovation, and align the workforce with national and global industry requirements.

All these demands led to the NEP 2020 which has made education more suitable in many ways such as:

(a) **Holistic and Multidisciplinary Learning**

One of the key outcomes of NEP 2020 is the promotion of holistic and multidisciplinary learning, which breaks away from the traditional rigid division of arts, science, and commerce streams. Earlier, students were confined to narrowly defined subject choices, often limiting their academic growth and career opportunities. NEP 2020 addresses this by encouraging flexibility, enabling learners to pursue combinations of subjects across disciplines such as blending life science with commerce, or physics with philosophy, or economics with computer science according to their interests and aspirations (Ministry of Education, 2020; NITI Aayog, 2021). This integrated approach fosters creativity, critical thinking, and the ability to translate theoretical knowledge into practical applications. For example, a student in life sciences may possess the expertise to develop a product but, in earlier systems, often lacked the entrepreneurial skills needed for commercialisation. By combining life sciences with commerce, such students can now gain insights into business strategies, marketing, and entrepreneurship, enabling them to transform innovations into viable products. This not only empowers individuals to become entrepreneurs but also contributes to national economic growth. This integrated approach not only fosters creativity, critical thinking, and problem-solving but also equips students with diverse skill sets needed for the complexities of the 21st-century workforce. By valuing both vocational and academic learning, the policy ensures that education nurtures well-rounded individuals capable of adapting to varied professional and life situations, ultimately aligning learning outcomes with global standards.

(b) Flexible Equity, Inclusion, and Lifelong Learning

NEP 2020 places strong emphasis on flexible equity, inclusion, and lifelong learning, addressing long-standing challenges such as school dropouts, gender disparities, and regional imbalances in access to education. Despite previous progress, many children, especially from marginalised and disadvantaged communities, were excluded from mainstream education due to socioeconomic barriers (UNESCO, 2021). The policy responds to this by introducing measures such as universal access to quality schooling, targeted support for underprivileged groups, gender-sensitive reforms, and the use of technology to bridge regional gaps. Furthermore, NEP 2020 envisions education as a continuous and lifelong process, ensuring opportunities for reskilling and upskilling at different stages of life to meet evolving social and economic needs. This inclusive framework not only guarantees "education for all" but also creates an equitable system where every learner, regardless of background, can thrive and contribute meaningfully to society.

4. New Education Policy (NEP) 2020 and its key features

The National Education Policy 2020 is a landmark reform in the Indian education system, introduced after more than three decades since the last major policy revisions of 1986 and its 1992 update. Initiated under the vision of the Government of India, particularly through the Ministry of Education (formerly MHRD), NEP 2020 was formulated to align India's education with the demands of the 21st century (Government of India, 2020). The policy emphasizes inclusivity, equity, quality, and flexibility while focusing on transforming both school and higher education. It moves beyond learning, seeking to nurture creativity, critical thinking, and problem solving abilities, thus preparing learners to thrive in a rapidly changing, knowledge driven global environment.

NEP 2020 also envisions a holistic and multidisciplinary approach to education, promoting vocational training, skill development, and lifelong learning opportunities. It aims to universalise education from school level to secondary level, strengthen foundational literacy and numeracy, and provide global exposure while preserving India's cultural and linguistic diversity (Government of India, 2020). By addressing persistent issues like dropouts, regional and gender disparities, and outdated curricula, NEP 2020 sets forth a comprehensive framework to make India a global knowledge hub and equip learners with the skills, values, and flexibility required for personal growth, national development, and global competitiveness.

The National Education Policy (NEP) 2020 lays strong emphasis on providing a holistic, flexible, and multidisciplinary education system that encourages creativity, innovation, and critical thinking among learners (Chandramana et al., 2020; Ashokkumar et al., 2025). The rigid barriers between arts, science, and commerce are dissolved to allow students the freedom to choose subjects across disciplines, catering to their interests and career goals. This holistic vision also integrates curricular, co-curricular, and extra-curricular activities, thereby focusing on the all round development of learners.

One of the key highlights of NEP 2020 is the focus on Foundational stage and Early Childhood Care and Education (ECCE). Recognizing the foundational importance of the early years, NEP 2020 ensures universal access to quality pre-primary education and introduces the 5+3+3+4 curricular and pedagogical structure, replacing the old 10+2 system. This structure is more aligned with cognitive stages of child development, providing a smooth transition from foundational learning to higher education. Additionally, the policy promotes the use of mother tongue or regional languages as the medium of instruction at least until Grade 5, to enhance conceptual understanding and strengthen cultural identity.

NEP 2020 also aims to mainstream vocational education from the school level, ensuring that at least 50% of learners get exposure to hands-on skills, internships, and apprenticeships by 2025. Complementing this, the National Mission on Foundational Literacy and Numeracy (NIPUN Bharat) has been launched to achieve universal literacy and numeracy by Grade 3, addressing one of the most pressing needs of the education system (Ministry of Education, 2021).

For higher education, the policy introduces a multiple entry exit system, allowing students to re-enter academic pathways with credits preserved through an Academic Bank of Credits (ABC). Furthermore, it emphasizes the integration of technology in teaching, learning, assessments, and governance, ensuring inclusivity, accessibility, and quality in education across the country. Together, these features position NEP 2020 as a forward looking framework to transform Indian education in line with global standards while addressing local needs.

5. Challenges in Implementation

The implementation of NEP 2020 faces several challenges despite its ambitious and visionary framework (Figure 2). One of the foremost issues is funding constraints and resource allocation. The policy envisions universal access to quality education, infrastructure improvement, and the establishment of research foundations, which demand substantial financial investment. However, the education sector in India has historically received less than the recommended 6% of GDP, creating a gap between policy goals and actual implementation (Tilak, 2019; Ministry of Education, 2020). Without adequate funding, many of the reforms, particularly in rural and underdeveloped areas, may remain only on paper.

With more than 1100 universities and 43,000 colleges and approx 16 lakhs teachers, till date India ensured on by 15% of gross enrollment ratio in higher education. NEP 2020 target is 50% by 2035. This means 3.5 times enhanchment in infrastructure and human resource (HR) in next 10 years. With an enhancement of 1.52% of GDP in education sector, this huge infrastructural and HR enhancement may be possible only with involvement of private entrepreneurship. But in that case affordability remains a challenge. The situation in school education is similar, with nearly 1.5 million schools and 9.6 million teachers catering to about 260 million students, resulting in a Gross Enrollment Ratio (GER) of around 51%. NEP 2020 target for school education is 100% GER. This means that there are more than 52 crores of students, approx 192 lakhs school teachers and 3.0 million schools. Therefore, GDP enhancement of 1.52% GDP may not be enough for the same.

The image was prepared using Napkin AI

Figure 2: The several major challenges in implementing NEP2020 including the funding constraints, Teacher Training, Regional disparities and Resistance to change etc.

Another major challenge is the training of teachers for new pedagogies. NEP 2020 calls for experiential learning, competency-based approaches, integration of vocational education, and use of technology. For this transformation to succeed, teachers must be equipped with modern teaching methodologies, digital literacy, and continuous professional development programmes. However, large scale teacher training is a daunting task in a diverse country like India, where teacher-student ratios are often imbalanced in many places, and resources for capacity building are limited.

Regional disparities in infrastructure also pose a significant obstacle. Urban areas may quickly adopt digital classrooms, flexible learning models, and vocational integration, but rural and remote regions still struggle with basic facilities like electricity, internet access, and adequate classrooms. These disparities could widen the existing educational gap, undermining the inclusive vision of NEP 2020 specially in the area of digital learning. Ensuring equity in access to technology and infrastructure remains a pressing concern.

Finally, resistance to change in traditional education structures creates another barrier. The shift from conventional single discipline specific learning to multidisciplinary and skill-oriented education requires a major cultural transformation in how education is perceived by institutions, parents, and students. Many stakeholders may resist changes such as multiple entry exit systems, the use of mother tongue as a medium of instruction, use of digital platforms or the dismantling of rigid academic streams. Overcoming these challenges requires strong political will, stakeholder participation, and phased implementation to make NEP 2020 a practical success.

6. Conclusion

The National Education Policy (NEP) 2020, launched under the leadership of Prime Minister Narendra Modi, is a landmark reform aimed at transforming India's human resource development into a globally competitive and knowledge driven system. Built upon the vision of "Transforming India," this policy breaks away from the rigid, outdated frameworks of earlier education policies and introduces holistic, flexible, and multidisciplinary approaches. With a focus on foundational literacy, skill development, digital learning, and research, NEP 2020 seeks to nurture innovation, creativity, and critical thinking while making education inclusive and accessible to all. Importantly, the policy reflects Government's vision of making India a global knowledge superpower, aligning with the aspirations of New India @75 and beyond. The outcomes of NEP 2020 are far-reaching integrating vocational training into schools, introducing the 5+3+3+4 structure, multidisciplinary approach, outcome based practical learning, strengthening research culture through the National Research Foundation, and enabling multiple entry exit pathways in higher education. These reforms bridge the gap between academic knowledge and employability, equipping students with skills needed for the 21st century economy. Moreover, emphasis on regional languages, early childhood care, and equity ensures education is rooted in inclusivity and cultural identity. However, the challenges of implementation cannot be ignored. Funding shortfalls, uneven infrastructure, teacher training gaps, and resistance to changing traditional systems remain pressing hurdles. For NEP 2020 to succeed, strong political will, sustained investment, and stakeholder collaboration are essential. In conclusion, while NEP 2020 under the Modi government lays a visionary roadmap for transforming India's educational landscape, its true success will depend on overcoming these implementation challenges and ensuring that its benefits reach every learner, from rural villages to global universities. Despite all the challenegs, one thing is clear that never earlier such a holistic approach for Indianisation of Education system was adopted. If the challenges are addressed at the level of stakeholders, there is no doubt that NEP 2020 shall bring a new dawn in the education system, awakening young minds making them self sufficient. Only then the dream of Hon'ble Prime Minister, Shri Narendra Modi ji's Vikshit Bharat 2047 will come true. NEP 2020 is not just a policy, it is a vision. It is we who are to act at an respective model to get the philosophy of NEP 2020. This is just the beginning; miles to go yet.

References

Ashokkumar, T., Raj, R. T., Rajadurai, A., Abishini, A. H., & Anchani, A. H. (2025). Analyzing the impact of the new educational policy 2020: A comprehensive review of India's educational reforms. Evaluation and Program Planning, 108, 102515. https://doi.org/10.1016/j.evalprogplan.2025.102515

Chandramana, S. B., & Kurien, A. (2020). Impact of New Education Policy 2020 on higher education. Figshare. Conference contribution. https://doi.org/10.6084/m9.figshare.13332413.v1

Erfan, M. (2024). The impact of cross-cultural management on global collaboration and performance. Asian Human Resource Management Review, 2(2). https://doi.org/10.60079/ahrmr.v2i2.261

Government of India. (2020). National Education Policy 2020. Ministry of Education, New Delhi.

Herlinawati, H., Marwa, M., Ismail, N., Junaidi, L., Liza, L. O., & Situmorang, D. D. B. (2024). The integration of 21st century skills in the curriculum of education. Heliyon, 10(15), e35148. https://doi.org/10.1016/j.heliyon.2024.e35148

Indian Express. (2021, September 22). Kasturirangan-led panel to develop new curriculum for schools. https://indianexpress.com

Kingdon, G. G. (2007). The progress of school education in India. Oxford Review of Economic Policy, 23(2), 168–195.

Ministry of Education. (2021). NIPUN Bharat: National Initiative for Proficiency in Reading with Understanding and Numeracy. Government of India, New Delhi.

Ministry of Education, Government of India. (2020). National Education Policy 2020. New Delhi: Government of India.

NITI Aayog. (2021). School Education Quality Index (SEQI) and policy implementation reports. Government of India, New Delhi.

Press Information Bureau. (2020, July 29). Cabinet approves National Education Policy 2020, paving way for transformational reforms in school and higher education systems in the country. Government of India.https://pib.gov.in/PressReleasePage.aspx?PRID=1642061

Tilak, J. B. G. (2003). Vocational education and training in Asia. In J. P. Keeves et al. (Eds.), International handbook of educational research in the Asia-Pacific region (Vol. 11, pp. 673–686). Springer. https://doi.org/10.1007/978-94-017-3368-7_46

Tira, N. F. (2021). Artificial intelligence (AI) in education: Using AI tools for teaching and learning process. Prosiding Seminar Nasional & Call for Paper STIE AAS.

UNESCO. (2012). Transforming technical and vocational education and training: Building skills for work and life.

UNESCO. (2021). Reimagining our futures together: A new social contract for education.

Vieriu, A. M., & Petrea, G. (2025). The impact of artificial intelligence (AI) on students' academic development. Education Sciences, 15(3), 343. https://doi.org/10.3390/educsci15030343

Yamin, M. (2019). Information technologies of 21st century and their impact on the society. International Journal of Information Technology, 11(4), 759–766. https://doi.org/10.1007/s41870-019-0035

20

Transforming India's Educational Landscape (2014–2025): A Decade of Change, A Future of Infinite Possibilities

Prof. (Dr.) Manpreet Singh Manna[1]

Since 2014, India has witnessed a transformational shift in education, led by the visionary leadership of Prime Minister Narendra Modi. With a strong resolve to build a **Viksit Bharat,** the country has reimagined and revitalised every layer of its educational ecosystem—unlocking opportunities, empowering millions, and laying the foundation for global leadership.

The decade saw a **60% increase in universities**—from 760 in 2014 to over 1,213 in 2024. More than 21% growth in colleges and the establishment of 42 new premier institutions—7 IITs, 8 IIMs, 16 IIITs, new AIIMS in the Northeast, and the first Central University in Ladakh—demonstrate an unwavering commitment to access and excellence.

School infrastructure dramatically improved. Electricity access rose from 53% to 91.8%, internet availability grew from 7.3% to 53.9%, and drinking water access reached 98.3%. Girls' toilet availability jumped from 30% to 91%, contributing to a **dropout rate decline from 9.1% to 1.5%**—an inspiring step toward inclusive education.

1. Chandigarh University, Gharuan, Mohali 140 413, (Punjab)

Digital empowerment has been a game-changer. Initiatives like **DIKSHA, SWAYAM, and PM eVidya** revolutionised access to quality content. Vocational education schools grew from under 1,000 in 2014 to nearly **30,000 by 2024**, and CBSE schools doubled to over 30,000. JEE and NEET exams are now conducted in **13 regional languages**, ensuring equitable learning opportunities.

In higher education, India's **Gross Enrollment Ratio (GER)** rose from 23.7% in 2014–15 to 28.4% in 2021–22. School-level GERs remain strong—93% at primary, 77% at secondary, and 56% at higher secondary levels. The **teacher-pupil ratio** improved from 42:1 to 24:1, and schemes like **RISE and HEFA** mobilized ₹ 1 lakh crore for infrastructure and innovation.

Focused interventions such as **Beti Bachao, Beti Padhao** led to a **23% rise in girls' STEM enrollment**. Dedicated scholarships, hostels, model schools, and outreach programmes ensured better inclusion for SC/ST/OBC communities, rural students, and girl children.

Defence education aligned with **Aatmanirbhar Bharat**, witnessing a 170% rise in production—from ₹ 46,429 crore in 2014–15 to ₹ 1.27 lakh crore in 2023–24. Innovation platforms like **iDEX and ADITI** offered up to ₹ 25 crore in funding. Defence corridors attracted over ₹ 8,600 crore in investment, solidifying India's stature in indigenous innovation.

At the heart of this transformation is **NEP 2020**, a bold blueprint for holistic, flexible, and future-ready education. With its 5+3+3+4 structure, focus on multilingualism, Academic Bank of Credits, digital learning, and global collaboration, it sets India on course to become a knowledge superpower.

As we look ahead, it is time to **recall our roots and ignite the spirit of "Swadeshi Shiksha: Desh Vapsi Ki Aur."** Let this be a national movement inviting our global scholars, innovators, and educators to return and co-create the future. The groundwork is laid. India is not just ready to lead—it is ready to shape the world.

21

Prime Minister Narendra Modi and India's Defence Transformation during the Period from 2014-2024

Dr. Mohammad Samir Hussain

Under the leadership of Prime Minister Narendra Modi, the Indian government has achieved remarkable advancement in the defence sector. The past decade, spanning from 2014 to 2024, can genuinely be referred to as the decade of defence transformation which is really very much significant from the national security point of view. Responding to the wide range of threats and challenges that our country face at present requires a proactive national security policy. This goal has been continuously met by the Modi administration, guaranteeing a secure, robust, and stable country.

Since 2014, the Indian government has undertaken number of initiatives aimed at strengthening India's overall military capability so as to effectively and efficiently deal with the myriad nature of threats and challenges in the coming decades of the 21st century. During this period, India has experienced a strategic shift in its strategy towards defence manufacturing, signifying a break from the reluctance and reliance characteristic of the period before 2014.

It is the Prime Minister Modi's firm believes that development and national security are closely connected to each other, which has driven the initiative of *Atmanirbhar Bharat* (self-reliance) in the defence sector. The present government took the right decision by converting Ordnance Factory Board into seven new Defence Public Sector Undertakings, out of which six are in profit. India's inaugural indigenous aircraft carrier, INS Vikrant, exemplifies the nation's increasing capabilities in indigenous manufacturing. So far, over more than 5000 items have been added to the defence indigenisation lists. Besides, 75 percent of defence capital acquisition budget earmarked for domestic production in the Financial Year 2025-26. Moreover, India's defence exports have increased from just ₹ 1,521 crore in 2016-17 to a whopping ₹ 23,622 crore in the financial year 2024-25.

The priority of the present government is to strengthen domestic capabilities and building a robust defence industrial ecosystem in our country. India has upgraded its armed forces by procuring cutting edge weaponry such as Rafale fighter jets and S-400 air defence systems. Indigenous systems like LCA Tejas and BrahMos have further enhanced capabilities. The integration of space-based Intelligence, Surveillance, and Reconnaissance (ISR) tools demonstrates India's preparedness for combat scenarios. Additionally, India's electronic warfare capabilities have been strengthened through the development of systems designed to disrupt enemy communications and radar operations. India's progress towards operational readiness has been made possible due to significant defence reforms initiated under his leadership. Under his leadership, the Government of India took decisive action of appointing a Chief of Defence Staff, which has not only enhanced coordination and decision-making among the services but also enables quicker responses to security threats and challenges.

Significant numbers of initiatives have been undertaken during his tenure to enhance the agility, technological orientation, and capability of the Indian military to deter or win conflicts in multi-domain operational setting. These initiatives also address a significant aspect of India's long-term ambition and self perception as a global power and a leading industrial nation.

22

Empowering Youth in India: A Policy Analysis of Prime Minister Narendra Modiji's Initiatives

Dr. N Vani Shree[1], Ms. Rajeswari H[2]

Introduction

The tenure of Sri Narendra Modi crosses a decade surpassing the former Prime Minister Smt. Indira Gandhi, as the Prime Minister of India or as Sri Modi likes himself to be addressed as 'Pradhan Sevak'. During his period, Sri. Modi has brought in several changes in the economy, foreign direct investments, legislative, administrative and brought in a huge global recognition to India. There is an abundant and overflowing boom in the growth of the cultural heritage of India, recognizing the country's diaspora and diversity. The nation's Pradhan Mantri aims in developing each and every diverse sector of the country. Several plans for developing the youth, women, and underprivileged classes are executed by him. This article prominently aims to explain about the contribution and role of the Hon'ble Prime Minister of India, Sri. Narendra

1. Completed BBA.LL.B (Hons.,) Programme at JSS Law College (Autonomous), Mysuru, Karnataka, India.
2. Principal @JSS Law College (Autonomous), Mysuru, Karnataka, India

Modiji's vision in the development of the youth of the nation. This essay delves into several problems faced by the youth such as unemployment, poverty, loan burdens and career dilemmas and how Sri. Modi as a leader mitigated it.

Modiji as a Student's Guide

PM Modi's youth-oriented initiatives are a strategic act understanding that the population of India is dominated by the youth. Yet, he is an empathetic leader who understands that the youth of this generation needs love and guidance. From the kids of the kindergarten to the Doctoral candidates, his initiatives aim in fulfilling the needs. The PM believed that proper nutrition is necessary for all the children and stressed on including protein rich millets in their diets. The Prime Minister informed that for an individual to progress in life, the importance of nutrition lies in what, when, how and why one eats, and also urged the children to focus on wellness[1]. Modiji is known to have a wide interest in motivating students and children all over India, he is known for his interactions and motivating talks to the growing and grownup generation of this nation. An interactive series known as 'Pariksha pe Charcha[2]' was conducted for advising students and parents on the importance of creating a stress free environment during exams. Prime Minister Modi was spotted engaging in a heartfelt conversation with students, carefully addressing their various concerns related to exams, including doubts they harbored, the stress that often accompanies such assessments, and the anxiety that can stem from academic pressures. Throughout this interaction, he skillfully maintained a lighthearted atmosphere filled with laughter and humor. His use of jokes and endearing gestures helped create a supportive environment, encouraging students to express themselves freely while alleviating some of the tension they faced.

1. https://www.pib.gov.in/PressReleasePage.aspx?PRID=2102683
2. https://secure.mygov.in/hi/ppc-2024/

Financial Assistance

1. Pradhan Mantri Uchchatar Shiksha Protsahan (PM-USP) Central Sector Scheme of Scholarship for College and University students[1]

The Ministry of Education's Department of Higher Education administers the "Pradhan Mantri Uchchatar Shiksha Protsahan (PM-USP) Central Sector Scheme of Scholarship for College and University Students" scholarship programme. The scheme's main goal is to give financially deserving students from low-income households support to cover some of their daily costs while they pursue higher education. Based on the outcomes of the Higher Secondary/Class 12th Board Examination, the scholarships are given out. A maximum of 82,000 new scholarships are awarded annually to students pursuing graduate or postgraduate degrees in colleges and universities, as well as to students enrolled in professional programmes like engineering, medicine, etc.

2. Prime Minister's Scholarship Scheme[2]

In order to promote higher technical and professional education for dependent wards of ex-servicemen and ex-Coast Guard personnel and their widows, the Ministry of Defense's Department of Ex-Servicemen Welfare launched the Prime Minister's Scholarship Scheme in the academic year 2006–07. Each academic year, 5500 wards or widows of ex-servicemen are chosen for the award (2750 boys and 2750 girls). The chosen students receive the scholarship money every year for a duration of one to five years, depending on how long the courses are permitted by the relevant regulatory organisations. The scholarship is worth ₹ 3000 for ladies and ₹ 2500 for boys per month.

1. https://www.myscheme.gov.in/schemes/csss-cus
2. https://www.myscheme.gov.in/schemes/pmss

3. The PM CARES for Children Scheme[1]

On May 29, 2021, the Hon'ble Prime Minister of India introduced the PM CARES for Children Scheme. It seeks to assist children who, beginning on March 11, 2020, lost both of their parents, legal guardians, adoptive parents, or surviving parents due to the COVID-19 epidemic. In addition to providing long-term, comprehensive care and protection, the scheme aims to empower children via education, promote their well-being through health insurance, and prepare them for self-sufficiency with financial assistance once they turn 23.

Skill Development Initiatives

Shri Narendra Modi has been widely recognized for his proactive initiatives aimed at addressing the challenges of unemployment in India. Understanding that traditional employment avenues alone may not be sufficient to meet the aspirations of a rapidly growing youth population, he has consistently focused on creating diverse and sustainable opportunities for skill enhancement and job creation. His vision goes beyond conventional job markets, emphasizing the need to prepare the youth for emerging sectors, entrepreneurship, and innovation-driven careers. Under his leadership, numerous policies and programmes have been introduced to strengthen skill development, promote self-reliance, and encourage employment in both organized and unorganized sectors.

Some of the flagship initiatives in this regard include:

1. **Skill India Mission[2]**

   Prime Minister Mr. Narendra Modi established the Skill India Mission in 2015 as part of his goal to assist India in becoming "Aatmanirbhar," or self-sufficient. The goal of this project was to design and carry out extensive

---

1. https://pmcaresforchildren.in/
2. https://www.ibef.org/government-schemes/skill-india

training programmes for skill development that would aid in closing the skills gap between industry demands and the nation's overall development.

Implementing curriculum-based skill training courses, where students would obtain certificates and endorsements from industry-recognized learning centers, was part of the Skill India programmes. Incorporating skill-based learning into the curriculum and establishing possibilities for both short-term and long-term skill training and employment were further aspects of the objective.

2. **Pradhan Mantri Kaushal Vikas Yojana (PMKVY)**[1]

   By offering financial incentives and rewards as well as high-quality training, the PMKVY plan seeks to boost the working efficiency of potential and current daily wage earners and to foster their aptitude for employable skills.

3. **Startup India and Stand-Up India**[2]

   Startup India is a flagship initiative of the Government of India, intended to catalyse startup culture and build a strong and inclusive ecosystem for innovation and entrepreneurship in India.

4. **Make in India**[3]

   The government of India launched the "Made in India" campaign to promote committed investments in manufacturing and to encourage businesses to design, produce, and assemble goods in India. The goal of the policy approach was to open up new industries

1. https://www.msde.gov.in/offerings/schemes-and-services/details/pradhan-mantri-kaushal-vikas-yojana-4-0-pmkvy-4-0-2021-ITO3ATMtQWa
2. https://www.startupindia.gov.in/
3. https://www.makeinindia.com

for foreign investment, build a modern and effective infrastructure, and foster an atmosphere that was favourable to investments.

5. **Atmanirbhar Bharat Abhiyan**[1]

   Fostering self-reliant industries and local enterprises to boost job creation, several internship opportunities were also given and many initiatives as such for skill development and Atmanirbhar Bharat. Through these initiatives, Prime Minister Modi has sought not only to provide immediate employment solutions but also to build a long-term frame-work for sustainable livelihoods and economic resilience among India's youth.

Conclusion

The youth of India represent the nation's greatest strategic resource, and the Modi administration's initiatives demonstrate a clear recognition of this fact. Through integrated policies spanning skills enhancement, structured employment creation, entrepreneurial facilitation, and expanded educational access the government has built a multitier framework aimed at converting demographic potential into economic and social strength. Measured outcomes, such as core scale skill training completions, millions of jobs through ELI and Rozgar Melas, and exponential startup growth, indicate that these policies are not merely aspirational, but operationally effective. However, continued evaluation, sector specific adjustments, and equitable regional implementation will remain essential to sustaining impact. If maintained with consistency and adaptability; these initiatives have the potential to transform India's youth into a globally competitive, innovation driven workforce paving the way for realising the vision of a Viksit Bharat by 2047.

---

1. https://www.india.gov.in/atmanirbhar-bharat-abhiyan

References

1. Press Information Bureau, Ministry of Skill Development & Entrepreneurship, Skill India Mission Empowers over 1.63 Crore Youth under PMKVY, (Apr. 2025), https://ddnews.gov.in/en/indias-skill-push-empowers-over-1-63-crore-youth-under-pmkvy.
2. Ministry of Rural Development, Deen Dayal Upadhyaya Grameen Kaushalya Yojana, https://en.wikipedia.org/wiki/Deen_Dayal_Upadhyaya_Grameen_Kaushalya_Yojana.
3. Atal Innovation Mission, NITI Aayog, Impact Report 2025, https://www.narendramodi.in/reader/skilling-india-s-youth-an-era-of-empowerment-under-pm-modi.
4. India Cabinet Approves $11.7 Bln Employment Incentives Plan to Create 35 Mln Jobs, Reuters (July 1, 2025), https://www.reuters.com/business/world-at-work/india-cabinet-approves-117-bln-employment-incentives-plan-create-35-mln-jobs-2025-07-01.
5. Press Information Bureau, Ministry of Personnel, Rozgar Melas Distribute 1 Million Appointment Letters to Youth, (May 2025), https://www.narendramodi.in/mobile/11-years-of-opportunity-inclusion-and-growth-under-pm-modi.
6. The Hindu, PM Internship Scheme Pilot Posts 1.27 Lakh Internships Across India (Dec. 2024), https://www.thehindu.com/news/national/pm-internship-scheme-rolled-out-on-pilot-basis-aims-to-provide-1-crore-internships-over-five-years/article68713887.ece.
7. Livemint, PM Internship Scheme Offers Stipends and Grants to Young Interns (Dec. 2024), https://www.livemint.com/companies/internship-companies-corporate-social-responsibility-employment-job-creation-government-cii-ficci-skills-11728887698799.html.
8. Startup India, Department for Promotion of Industry & Internal Trade, Annual Startup Report 2025, https://en.wikipedia.org/wiki/Startup_India.
9. Seetha Mahadevan, Under-30 Entrepreneurs Created Over 64,000 Jobs in India, Raised $5.2 Billion in Funding: Hurun–Avendus Report, Econ. Times (July 23, 2025), https://economictimes.indiatimes.com/tech/startups/under-30-entrepreneurs-created-over-64000-jobs-in-india-raised-5-2-billion-in-funding-hurun-avendus-report/articleshow/122640013.cms

10. Atal Innovation Mission, NITI Aayog, AIC Impact Review 2025, https://en.wikipedia.org/wiki/Atal_Innovation_Mission.
11. Ministry of Education, One Nation, One Subscription & Vidyalaxmi Scheme Report 2025, https://www.narendramodi.in/prime-minister-narendra-modi-partici-pates-in-viksit-bharat-young-leaders-dialogue-2025-at-bharat-mandapam-589800.

23

The Ascent of Narendra Modi: A Transformational Journey Since 2014

Prof. Nagaraj Ramrao[1]

Introduction: The ascent of Narendra Modi to the position of Prime Minister in May 2014 marked a pivotal moment in India's political and developmental landscape. With a strong electoral mandate—securing 282 Lok Sabha seats, the highest by any party in 30 years—and a vision encapsulated in "Sabka Saath, Sabka Vikas, Sabka Vishwas, Sabka Prayas," the Modi-led government embarked on a transformational journey to redefine governance, the economy, foreign policy, and India's global standing.

1. Governance Redefined: Transparency, Efficiency, and Digitalization

From the outset, the government prioritized transparency, efficiency, and digitalization. The flagship **Digital India** programme, launched in 2015, aimed to transform India into a digitally empowered society by connecting over 250,000 villages with high-speed internet. By 2025, internet penetration in rural India had surged to over 60%, with more than 900 million users nationwide. The **Pragati Platform** enabled real-time

1. Vice Chancellor, Mohan Babu University, Tirupati, vc@mbu.asia

monitoring of over 500 major projects across ministries and states, reducing average delays by 30%. To modernize the civil service, **Mission Karmayogi**, launched in 2020, enrolled over 3.3 million government officials in a digital learning ecosystem, enhancing administrative efficiency. Faceless tax assessments under the Income Tax Act and GST simplified compliance and reduced corruption, increasing tax revenue collections by 25% between 2017 and 2023.

2. Economic Reforms: Building a $5 Trillion Economy

India's nominal GDP grew from around $2.1 trillion in 2014 to more than $3.7 trillion in 2023, targeting $5 trillion by 2025. The introduction of the **Goods and Services Tax (GST)** in 2017 unified over 17 indirect taxes across states and benefited 1.4 million registered businesses. Monthly GST collections crossed ₹1.5 lakh crore post-2021. The **Insolvency and Bankruptcy Code (IBC)** streamlined corporate insolvency resolution, recovering assets worth ₹4.5 lakh crore. The **Make in India** initiative boosted manufacturing's GDP share from 16% to nearly 18% and attracted over $300 billion in foreign direct investment from 2014 to 2023. The startup ecosystem flourished under **Startup India**, with over 90,000 startups launched, positioning India as the third-largest home to unicorns globally by 2025. Production Linked Incentive (PLI) schemes incentivized investments exceeding ₹2.5 lakh crore across sectors like electronics and pharmaceuticals, further strengthening the manufacturing base. The country's **Ease of Doing Business** ranking improved significantly from 142nd in 2014 to 63rd in 2019.

3. Social Welfare and Inclusive Growth: Empowering the Marginalised

Social welfare schemes under Modi's tenure emphasized direct benefit transfers and last-mile delivery. The **Jan Dhan**

Yojana opened more than 470 million bank accounts, facilitating over ₹15 lakh crore in DBT transfers by 2024. The **Ujjwala Yojana** distributed over 90 million LPG connections, reducing indoor air pollution and saving an estimated 120,000 lives annually. The **Swachh Bharat Mission** constructed over 110 million toilets and declared 705 districts open-defecation free by 2019. **Ayushman Bharat**, launched in 2018, insured more than 540 million beneficiaries with free health coverage up to ₹5 lakh per family yearly. Additionally, **PM- KISAN** transferred ₹1.2 lakh crore directly to 110 million farmers. Affordable housing under the **PM Awas Yojana** has delivered over 11 million homes since inception.

4. Infrastructure Revolution: Building Modern India

India witnessed a massive infrastructure push. The **Bharatmala Project** targeted 83,000 km of roads by 2025, with over 35,000 km completed by 2024. The **Sagarmala Project** enhanced port capacities to 2.5 billion tonnes. The **Gati Shakti** platform coordinated infrastructure projects worth ₹100 lakh crore across ministries. The **Smart Cities Mission** developed 111 smart cities with investments exceeding ₹2 lakh crore. Indian Railways achieved over 70% electrification, introduced 44 Vande Bharat semi-high-speed trains, and redeveloped 1,200 stations. The **UDAN** scheme boosted regional connectivity by launching 500+ routes linking over 80 smaller cities, increasing domestic air travel by 30%.

5. Digital and Technological Advancement: Leading the Fintech Revolution

Digitally, India became a global leader. The **Unified Payments Interface (UPI)** grew from zero transactions in 2016 to over 10 billion monthly transactions worth ₹20 lakh crore by 2025. Aadhaar coverage reached 1.3 billion IDs, enabling streamlined welfare distribution. The rapid **5G rollout** covered

70% of urban and 40% of rural areas by mid-2025, catalysing AI and IoT adoption. India's **India Stack** and **JAM Trinity** (**Jan Dhan-Aadhaar-Mobile**) became global models for digital governance, influencing countries like Nigeria and Brazil.

6. National Security and Strategic Diplomacy: A Strong and Assertive India

On national security, decisive actions such as the **2016 surgical strikes** and the **2019 Balakot airstrike** signalled India's zero tolerance for cross-border terrorism. The government revoked **Article 370** in 2019, fully integrating Jammu & Kashmir into India's legal framework and investing ₹1.5 lakh crore into the region. Defence indigenization increased domestic production from 40% to over 70%, with FDI limits in defence raised from 26% to 74%. India strengthened strategic partnerships through the QUAD and expanded defence exports from ₹3,000 crore in 2014 to ₹13,000 crore in 2023.

7. Environmental Sustainability: Leading Green Growth

Environmental progress includes India's leadership in the **International Solar Alliance** (**ISA**), which mobilised over 100 countries to invest $1 trillion in solar energy by 2030. Solar capacity reached 120 GW by 2025. Initiatives like **Ujjwala 2.0** and an aggressive **electric vehicle push** saw over 20 million EVs registered, with annual sales growing 40%. The **National Hydrogen Mission** (**2021**) set ambitious targets for green hydrogen production. India increased its tiger population to over 3,000 by 2022 and expanded forest cover by 5% since 2014, fulfilling Paris Agreement targets ahead of schedule and pledging net-zero emissions by 2070.

8. Education, Youth, and Skilling: Investing in the Future

In education, the **National Education Policy** (**NEP**) **2020** introduced multi-lingual education and vocational training reforms, training 1.5 million teachers. The **Skill India Mission** certified 90 million youth, enhancing employability across sectors. **PM SHRI Schools** upgraded over 15,000 institutions to model standards. Higher education saw over 100 international collaborations by 2024.

9. Pandemic Response and Resilience: Managing a National Crisis

India's response to the COVID-19 pandemic demonstrated robust crisis management. The world's largest vaccination campaign delivered over 2.2 billion doses by 2023, achieving 85% adult coverage. The **Atmanirbhar Bharat** stimulus infused ₹20 lakh crore into the economy, representing nearly 10% of GDP, supporting MSMEs and households. The **CoWIN platform** enabled seamless vaccination registration and certification. India also emerged as a global vaccine manufacturing hub, producing 60% of the world's COVID-19 vaccines.

10. Looking Ahead: Vision for Amrit Kaal (2022–2047)

The government's **Vision for Amrit Kaal** aims to make India a developed, digitally-first, and green economy by 2047. Targets include doubling farmers' incomes by 2030, universal broadband access, leading global AI innovation, increasing women's workforce participation from 25% to 35%, and investing over ₹1,00,00,000 crore in infrastructure.

11. Challenges and Areas for Improvement

Despite tremendous progress, challenges remain. The unemployment rate, especially among youth, remains high fluctuating between 7-9% overall and peaking over 23% for young adults. Approximately 50% of farmers continue to face distress despite financial support. Social polarization and concerns over freedom of expression, as reflected in India's

150th rank in the 2024 World Press Freedom Index, require attention to maintain social harmony and democratic values.

12. Strengthening Federalism and Cooperative Governance

Federalism has been strengthened through cooperative institutions like the GST Council, which has held over 40 meetings resolving tax disputes for 130 million taxpayers. The Smart Cities Mission and Jal Jeevan Mission have brought transformative urban and rural development, with 70% of villages now having potable water access.

13. India's Global Footprint: Rising as a Major Power

India's Global Footprint: Rising as a Major Power

Since Narendra Modi took office as Prime Minister in 2014, India has dramatically expanded its role on the global stage, asserting itself as a major geopolitical and economic power. This transformation is driven by a strategic foreign policy that balances traditional alliances with emerging partnerships, a strong emphasis on multilateralism, and active engagement in global governance institutions.

Strengthening Multilateral Platforms: BRICS and Beyond

India has leveraged its membership in **BRICS** (Brazil, Russia, India, China, South Africa) to deepen economic cooperation and promote a multipolar world order. BRICS, representing nearly 42% of the global population and about 23% of the world GDP (2023 figures), serves as a critical forum where India has:

- **Pushed for reforms in global governance institutions** such as the United Nations Security Council and the International Monetary Fund, advocating for greater representation of emerging economies.

- **Promoted economic cooperation** through the New Development Bank (NDB), headquartered in Shanghai but with a significant role for India. The NDB has financed infrastructure and sustainable development projects worth billions of dollars across member nations, boosting India's infrastructure agenda.
- **Facilitated knowledge sharing and collaboration** on inno-vation, digital economy, and sustainable development goals.
- Played an active role in expanding BRICS outreach, inviting key emerging economies like Argentina, Egypt, Ethiopia, Iran, Saudi Arabia, and the UAE to become new members in 2023 — reflecting India's vision of a broad, inclusive coalition of Global South nations.

Championing South-South Cooperation

India has emerged as a leader of **South-South cooperation,** promoting development partnerships with Asia, Africa, and Latin America based on shared experiences and mutual benefit rather than traditional donor-recipient dynamics. This approach reflects India's own development journey and commitment to inclusive growth.

Key aspects include:

- **India-Africa-Relations:**

  India is Africa's 3rd largest trading partner, with bilateral trade crossing USD 85 billion in 2023. Through initiatives like the India-Africa Forum Summit and the Pan-African e-Network project, India has enhanced technology transfer, education, and health infrastructure on the continent. India also provides concessional lines of credit and capacity-building programmes for African nations.

- **Development Assistance and Capacity Building:**

  India's Development Partnership Administration (IDPA) manages technical cooperation programmes across 65+ countries, offering training, scholarships, and development finance in areas such as agriculture, IT, health, and renewable energy. India has extended over USD 30 billion in concessional credit lines since 2004, supporting infrastructure and social sector projects worldwide.

- **Climate and Energy Leadership:**

  India's launch of the **International Solar Alliance (ISA)** in 2015 with over 120 member countries aims to harness solar energy for sustainable development among tropical countries in the Global South. ISA demonstrates India's commitment to climate action while fostering South-South technological cooperation.

- **Trade and Connectivity:**

  Through regional initiatives like the **South Asian Association for Regional Cooperation (SAARC), Bay of Bengal Initiative for Multi-Sectoral Technical and Economic Cooperation (BIMSTEC)**, and **Act East Policy,** India has expanded trade, cultural ties, and infrastructure connectivity with neighbouring and extended regions, promoting shared prosperity.

Strategic Autonomy and Global Partnerships

India's foreign policy under Modi has emphasized **strategic autonomy,** balancing close partnerships with the US, European Union, Japan, and Australia (through frameworks like the Quad), while maintaining strong ties with Russia and engaging with China through diplomacy and competition.

- India's growing defence exports, valued at over USD 1

billion annually, bolster its image as an emerging global arms supplier.

- As Chair of the **G20 in 2023**, India highlighted issues critical to developing countries including sustainable development, digital economy governance, and equitable access to vaccines and climate finance.
- India's active engagement with global bodies like the **Shanghai Cooperation Organisation (SCO)** and **ASEAN Regional Forum** demonstrates its multifaceted approach to diplomacy.

14. Youth Aspirations and Cultural Renaissance

India's youthful population—over 65% under 35—drives a cultural renaissance. The **Skill India** mission has certified 90 million youth, and the startup ecosystem boasts over 120 unicorns valued at $300 billion. Cultural initiatives like **Azadi Ka Amrit Mahotsav** engaged millions in celebrating India's heritage, while regional language education has increased by 20% since 2020, reinforcing linguistic diversity alongside modernisation.

Conclusion

Over the last eleven years, the Modi government has reshaped India's state and society— transforming welfare delivery, driving economic reforms, advancing digital governance, and asserting India's role on the global stage. While challenges such as unemployment, agrarian distress, and social tensions persist, the foundations laid through comprehensive policy action promise a dynamic, digital, and developed India in the decades ahead.

24

Bharatiya Chetanā and the Decade of Dharma: Reimagining India's Knowledge Traditions in the Era of Transformative Leadership

Prof. (Dr.) Narasingha Charan Panda[1]

The transformation that India has experienced in this past decade goes beyond the change of regime in a political entity and is more of a civilisational being arriving at its own spirit (chetanā) (Chatterjee, 2011). The same has come to inhabit the phenomenal and visionary leadership of the Hon'ble Prime Minister Shri Narendra Modi ji, whose tenure is not only a time of governance but of renewal of the Indian identity and thought and self-sustenance. As documented in the earlier volume *Pradhan Mantri to Pradhan Sewak: Modi's Quest for a Vibrant India* (Garg, 2015), the foundational years of Shri Modi ji's leadership reflected a grounded vision of service-oriented governance and nation-first commitment. That vision, rooted in grassroots empowerment and ethical leadership, has since evolved into a comprehensive national movement that is civilisational in scope and futuristic in aspiration (Goyal, 2022).

Being a Sanskrit and Indian Knowledge Systems scholar and currently endowed with the mandate of leading a central

1. Vice Chancellor, Central University of Odisha

university in one of the most culturally rich yet educationally longing pockets in India, Koraput in Odisha, I feel this decade is going to be the decade of restorative dharma. The classical meaning of the word dharma is that which promotes. Over the last decade, there has been a revival of that sustaining spirit in Indian policies, education, languages, as well as at the grassroot level governance (Sharma & Ram, 2025).

The drafting and the initiating of the *National Education Policy 2020 (NEP 2020)* is one of the most philosophically deep and futuristic documents that have come to implementation during this time. It makes Indian schooling meet the ancient holistic criteria *samyak jñāna*, *samyak karma*, and *samyak bhāvanā* (Gope et al., 2025). In contrast to the previous model, which mimicked the Western paradigms, NEP 2020 acknowledges *Bharatiya* epistemology as fundamental and legislates the classical languages, which since the previous model is not being treated as dead relics but as repositories of scientific, ethical, religious, and metaphysical wisdom (Ministry of Education, 2020).

This change of policy has not been symbolic, taking into consideration that it has effected (translated into) actual change in Indian classrooms and institutions. Multilanguage is no longer being discouraged. Those that used to pass off mother-tongue teaching are now using it as one of the means of cognitive excellence. In Sanskrit, universities are going multidisciplinary, and there is use of technology to restore ancient commentaries, oral traditions, and manuscripts (Vyas, 2023). The *Aspirational District Programme*, *PM SHRI Schools*, and *Digital India* programmes by the Modi government have opened up new avenues of opportunities to the crop of people who had no access to mainstream academia, particularly the rural and tribal hamlets of our heartland (Sakhamuri & Sanagani, 2024). Recent field-based research has also highlighted these shifts, particularly in the teacher education landscape of Odisha, where prospective English educators are increasingly engaging with multilingualism, pedagogical reform, and NEP-led institutional realignment (Suar et al., 2025). The gap between the policy and the reality on the ground is slowly closing—online access to platforms such as *DIKSHA*, availability of vernacular on digital platforms, and growing investment in infrastructure and faculty development are slowly playing a role in closing the gap between the policy intent and the reality (Gupta & Saranya, 2024).

We have seen that at the Central University of Odisha, the youth of tribal students get in touch with Indian philosophy, ethics, and works of literature, being inspired by the *Ramayana*, *Mahabharata*, *Vedas*, and *Upanishad* writings. They are now viewing themselves as being not mere recipients of knowledge, but co-producers of knowledge, according to the Indic world-view of learning as self-realisation (*svādhyāya*) (Pandey, 2024). It is this sense of ownership and pride which is probably the most important change experienced in this decade. When the Prime Minister expressed *Panch Pran*—freedom to free the colonial mindsets, pride in heritage, unity, being conscious of our duty and national development (Singh, 2023) —he was really echoing back to the 3000-year-old idealism in Sanskrit described as *"Bahujana hitāya bahujana sukhāya"*—the welfare and happiness of all. It is a civilisational requirement that is being liberated to be a modernised 21st-century India.

This is not just the era of economic development, but this is the period of spiritual awakening (Fogel, 2000). Through education, culture, and awareness, the Bharatiya values that have been missing through the ages are being resurrected, and this is bringing in a *Viksit Bharat*—An India that does not lead the world based on wealth but wisdom and compassion and character (Singh et al., 2024). I wholeheartedly give my support to this publishing project, which is interested in documenting the national pathway, *Pradhan Mantri to Pradhan Sevak*, *vikas* (development) to *sanskriti* (cultural rootedness). May this record stand, not only as a record but, as the record of a struggle of an Indian nation upflung in her own light—स्वयं प्रभा.

References

Chatterjee, P. (2011). Democracy and economic transformation in India. In S. Ruparelia, S. Reddy, J. Harriss, & S. Corbridge (Eds.), *Understanding India's new political economy: A great transformation?* (pp. 17–34). Routledge.

Fogel, R. W. (2000). *The fourth great awakening and the future of egalitarianism*. University of Chicago Press.

Garg, A. (Ed.). (2015). *Pradhan Mantri to Pradhan Sewak: Modi's quest for a vibrant India*. Gyan Books Pvt. Ltd.

Gope, L., Vajpayee, A., & Jha, P. (2025). Rediscovering the roots of ancient Indian pedagogical tools for quality education. *People, 2*(1).

Goyal, M. (2022). A new empowering India under leadership of PM Modi: Promises and reality. *Prosperity: Journal of Society and Empowerment, 2*(1), 49–62.

Gupta, S. K., & Saranya, T. S. (2024). Navigating the digital frontier: The unique challenges and opportunities of education in India. *Pedagogy and Education Management Review, 4*(18), 4–24.

Ministry of Education. (2020). *National Education Policy 2020*. Government of India. https://www.education.gov.in

Pandey, R. (2024). Synthesis of educational philosophy with Indian culture and traditional ethos: A framework for holistic development. *Nolegein Journal of Business Ethics, Ethos and CSR, 7*(2).

Sakhamuri, H., & Sanagani, V. (2024). Role of NITI Aayog. In *SDGs in the Asia and Pacific Region* (p. 447).

Sharma, S., & Ram, Y. (2025). Revitalizing indigenous languages: Analyzing key factors and strategies in the context of NEP 2020. *International Journal of Advanced Research and Multidisciplinary Trends (IJARMT), 2*(2), 348–355.

Singh, A. K., Mishra, S., Sethi, R., Arora, S., & Ansari, C. (2024). Three Vs in the context of ancient Indian tradition: Foundation of Viksit Bharat 2047. *International Journal of Research in Multidisciplinary Studies (IJRMS)*. Bharati Vidyapeeth's Institute of Computer Applications and Management (BVICAM), New Delhi.

Singh, V. K. (2023). 'Aazadi Ka Amrit Mahotsav' to vision for 'Amrit Kaal': Exploring the major issues in law and policy transformation in India. *SRMUH Law Review*, *1*(1).

Suar, G. B., Behera, R. R., Rout, R. K., Patra, S., Panda, P., & Sethi, P. (2025, April). English language and pedagogical competency of prospective English teachers: Insights and challenges from teacher education institutes in Odisha, India. *Frontiers in Education*, *10*, 1517466. https://doi.org/10.3389/feduc.2025.1517466

Vyas, M. S. (2023). Sanskrit in modern context: Exploring the use and revival of Sanskrit in contemporary society, including its role in education, literature, and arts. *Revista Review Index Journal of Multidisciplinary*, *3*(2), 1–10.

25

Narendra Modi: A Leader with a Humanitarian Soul

Dr. Naresh Kumar Tiwari, Vijnana Bharti[1]

Introduction: A Man of Many Dimensions

Narendra Modi, the Prime Minister of India, is not just a political figure but a symbol of resilience, compassion, and transformative leadership. His persona reflects strength forged by adversity and a heart touched deeply by the struggles of the common people...

1. Humble Beginnings: A Childhood of Empathy and Struggle

Born on 17th September 1950 in Vadnagar, Gujarat, Narendra Modi hailed from a modest family. His father was a tea vendor, and young Modi often helped him sell tea at the local railway station...

2. Inspired by Swami Vivekananda: Service Before Self

Swami Vivekananda's teachings deeply influenced Narendra Modi. The ideals of selfless service, spiritual discipline, and national pride became the foundation of his character...

1. Madhya Bharat Prant, Vice-Chancellor SAM Global University

3. Service in Calamity: Leadership with a Human Touch

Modi's humanitarian approach was vividly evident in times of disasters like the Gujarat Earthquake (2001), Uttarakhand Floods (2013), and COVID-19 pandemic (2020)...

4. Inclusive Policies for Every Citizen

Modi's governance philosophy revolves around the slogan 'Sabka Saath, Sabka Vikas, Sabka Vishwas, Sabka Prayas' — inclusive development with collective trust and effort...

5. A Global Humanitarian Leader

Narendra Modi's humanitarian outlook is not limited to national boundaries. He initiated global disaster relief efforts and introduced Yoga as a wellness tool for humanity...

6. Technology for the Common Man

Modi believes in using technology as a bridge, not a barrier. His digital policies are designed with humanitarian intent — to empower, not to exclude...

7. Environment and Sustainable Compassion

Modi's love for nature stems from cultural roots. He considers nature sacred and has led multiple green missions like the International Solar Alliance and Swachh Bharat Abhiyan...

8. Sensitive towards Youth, Children and Elders

Modi's policies often address emotional and practical needs of all age groups through initiatives like Pariksha Pe Charcha, Fit India Movement, and senior citizen schemes...

9. A Leader Who Listens: Direct Public Engagement

Modi revolutionized political communication in India through initiatives like Mann Ki Baat and NaMo App which connect him directly with the people...

10. Grace Under Criticism

Despite harsh criticism, Modi never reacts with bitterness. His response is rooted in dignity, silence, or constructive action...

11. Personal Simplicity, Public Responsibility

Modi lives a life of discipline, austerity, and self-reliance. He continues to maintain a deep connection with his roots and leads by example...

12. A Role Model for the Youth

Narendra Modi is admired for his self-discipline, work ethic, nationalism, clean image, and reform mindset...

13. A Cultural Guardian

While being forward-looking, Modi holds deep respect for Indian culture and traditions, reflected in initiatives like the Ram Mandir and Kashi Vishwanath Corridor...

14. Global Recognition as a Humanitarian Statesman

He has received numerous international honours such as the UN Champion of the Earth Award and highest civilian awards from multiple countries...

Conclusion: The Guardian of Humanity

Narendra Modi's journey — from a tea seller to the most powerful democratic leader in the world — is not just about ambition, but about purpose, empathy, and service...

26

An Epoch of Transformation: Eleven Years of Prime Minister Narendra Modi's Leadership

Dr. Priyesh P. Gandhi[1]

In the grand tapestry of India's civilisational journey, certain epochs shine with an unmistakable radiance—moments when the nation's destiny takes a decisive turn towards renewal and resurgence. The past eleven years under the stewardship of Hon'ble Prime Minister Shri Narendra Modi represent such an epoch: a period where governance has transcended administration to become a mission, and leadership has risen beyond politics to embody the collective dreams of over a billion people.

Reawakening the Social Spirit

From the sweeping vision of *Swachh Bharat Abhiyan* to the compassion embodied in *Ujjwala Yojana* and the life-saving shield of *Ayushman Bharat*, the Modi era has been defined by a deep engagement with the needs of the common citizen. In rural hamlets and urban sprawls alike, these initiatives have uplifted lives, restored dignity, and rekindled hope. The *Digital India*

1. Provost (Vice Chancellor), Sigma University, Vadodara.

movement has brought the hum of technology to the remotest corners, empowering students, farmers, and entrepreneurs alike. More than schemes, these have been instruments of social transformation—bridging divides, empowering women, and giving voice to the marginalised.

The Economic Renaissance

Economically, these eleven years have witnessed India's ascent as one of the most dynamic major economies. Reforms like the Goods and Services Tax (GST) have woven a unified market across the land, while the Insolvency and Bankruptcy Code has restored financial discipline and investor confidence. Infrastructure—be it expressways, ports, airports, or freight corridors—has expanded at a pace and scale unmatched in the republic's history. This is not mere construction of roads and buildings, but the laying of arteries through which the lifeblood of commerce, industry, and opportunity flows.

Manufacturing and Self-Reliance

The clarion call of *Make in India* and the structured incentives under the Production Linked Incentive (PLI) schemes have heralded a new industrial dawn. In sectors from electronics to defence, India has moved steadily from being a consumer to a creator. The manufacturing floor has once again become a crucible of innovation, ambition, and employment—turning the idea of *Atmanirbhar Bharat* from aspiration to action.

Diplomacy with Purpose

On the world stage, Prime Minister Modi has woven a diplomatic narrative where India speaks with both moral conviction and strategic clarity. From leading climate dialogues to voicing the aspirations of the Global South, India's position has been one of constructive leadership. Engagements in G20,

BRICS, QUAD, and bilateral partnerships have been marked by a rare blend of pragmatism and principle. The world has come to see India not merely as a rising power, but as a civilisational force offering balance, stability, and vision.

The Legacy of an Era

As we stand at the threshold of *Amrit Kaal*, the imprint of these eleven years is indelible—a Bharat that is more confident, self-reliant, technologically adept, socially inclusive, and globally respected. Prime Minister Modi's leadership has been akin to a sculptor chiselling away at the constraints of the past to reveal the possibilities of the future.

History will remember this era not only for the milestones achieved but for the spirit it rekindled—a belief that India's time is not just coming, it is here.

27

A Decade and Beyond: 11 Years of Achievements at SGPGIMS, Lucknow

Dr. Radha Krishan Dhiman[1]

Over the past eleven years of Prime Minister Shri Narendra Modi ji's leadership, India has undergone a profound transformation in healthcare delivery, research, and medical innovation. I have been privileged to witness how this enabling ecosystem has empowered institutions like the Sanjay Gandhi Postgraduate Institute of Medical Sciences (SGPGIMS), Lucknow, to dream bigger, expand faster, and serve society better. Established in 1984, when the foundation stone was laid by the then President of India, Shri Neelam Sanjeeva Reddy, SGPGIMS has since grown into one of the country's foremost centers of medical excellence, combining patient care, research, and academic leadership. A major milestone in our recent journey was the institute's recognition with the **prestigious NAAC A++ accreditation (2024)** — the highest rating awarded nationally. This was accompanied by an improvement in our **NIRF ranking to 5th place (2025)**, affirming SGPGIMS's standing among India's leading medical institutions. These recognitions validated our consistent pursuit of excellence across academics, research, patient care, and governance.

---

1. Director, Sanjay Gandhi Postgraduate Institute of Medical Sciences (SGPGIMS), Lucknow, President, AIIMS Patna, Recipient of Padma Shri and Dr. B.C. Roy National Award.

The story of expansion began with the establishment of the **Apex Trauma Centre (2018)**, the first Level-1 Trauma Centre in Uttar Pradesh, envisioned as a state-of-the-art hub for round-the-clock trauma management, rehabilitation, and emergency response. The **Naveen OPD Complex (2018)**, constructed the same year, was designed to improve patient convenience, accessibility, and workflow. It has since been upgraded with dedicated sample collection areas, escalators, PR counters, and advanced digital infrastructure, reflecting the Government's vision of "ease of living" for citizens.

The **COVID-19 pandemic (2020)** tested healthcare institutions worldwide, and SGPGIMS rose to the challenge with determination. We established the **Rajdhani COVID Hospital (2020),** the first dedicated apex-level COVID facility in the state, equipped with a 20,000-liter liquid oxygen plant and over 1,100 oxygen cylinders. SGPGIMS played a central role in training doctors and paramedics, conducting virtual ICU rounds for 52 medical colleges, and guiding the state's response. I also had the privilege of serving as Chairman of the State Advisory Boards for COVID and Mucormycosis. These efforts demonstrated how timely government support and institutional preparedness could save lives at scale.

In the post-pandemic years, SGPGIMS entered a new phase of growth. The **Emergency Medical and Renal Transplant Centre (2022)** was inaugurated as a cutting-edge facility, housing a 210-bedded Emergency Medicine Department and 348-bedded Departments of Nephrology and Urology with Renal Transplantation facility, a Digital Subtraction Angiography (DSA) lab, a CT scan and a dedicated Renal ICU.

In **2024**, several transformative initiatives came to life. The **Advanced Diabetic Centre (2024)** was launched, offering multi-disciplinary care across endocrinology, nephrology, ophthalmology, neurology, Hepatology and diabetic foot management to the patients with diabetes mellitus. This centre, along with the Tele-ICU facility and the Saloni Heart Centre–Phase I, was inaugurated in the august presence of Hon'ble Chief Minister of Uttar Pradesh, Shri Yogi Adityanath Ji, whose encouragement and blessings provided strong impetus to our mission of delivering advanced healthcare to the people of the state. The **Saloni Heart Centre – Phase I (2024)** began operations with a 30-bedded unit, 6-bedded ICU, and an operation theatre dedicated to children born with congenital heart disease. That same year, **nine new departments (2024)** were created — Paediatric Endocrinology, Infectious Diseases, Orthopaedics, Telemedicine and Digital Health, Paediatric Urology, Paediatric Nephrology, Paediatric CVTS, Head and Neck Surgery, and Hepatology — reflecting a broadening of specialisation and academic depth.

Collaboration between SGPGIMS, the Software Technology Parks of India (STPI), and the Department of IT and Infotech (2024) is fostering innovation in medical electronics and digital healthcare solutions. Already, 53 start-ups are on board 35 focused on product development and 50 on prototypes, showcasing how academia and technology incubation can power *Atmanirbhar Bharat.*

The **Rain Basera Project (2024)**, with a sanctioned budget of ₹50 crores, is another milestone aimed at improving patient welfare, providing accommodation for over 1,000 attendants. Plans for a new OPD complex, multilevel parking facilities, faculty housing, and resident hostels (2025 onward) are also underway, ensuring comprehensive institutional growth.

In **2025**, our focus has continued to expand. Phase II of the **Saloni Heart Centre (2025)** is underway and will add 200 more beds exclusively for children born with congenital heart disease. Simultaneously, the **Advanced Pediatric Centre (ongoing, 2025)** is progressing rapidly and, when complete, will house 575 beds across 24 departments in two phases, consolidating SGPGIMS's role as a national leader in pediatric health.

Our human resource base has been equally strengthened. By 2025, 113 faculty members have been recruited through the last six advertisements, and the institute is preparing to advertise 220 new faculty positions. Parallel to non-faculty posts, 1,870 selected and 1,560 already joined. An additional 1,479 non-faculty posts (2025) are under recruitment, reflecting the scale of institutional expansion.

At every stage of this journey, the consistent support of the State Government under the dynamic leadership of Hon'ble Chief Minister Shri Yogi Adityanath Ji has been invaluable. His presence at major inaugurations, encouragement for patient-centric projects, and vision for strengthening Uttar Pradesh's healthcare infrastructure have complemented the transformative policies of the Hon'ble Prime Minister, creating a powerful Centre–State synergy. The recently sanctioned Rain Basera Project, a compassionate initiative conceived under his guidance, will provide affordable accommodation for over 1,000 patients and their attendants, reflecting his commitment to patient welfare and dignity during treatment.

In my experience, none of this progress would have been possible without the enabling national policies and consistent encouragement provided by the State and the Central Government. The past eleven years have empowered SGPGIMS to expand its footprint, embrace innovation, and serve with greater compassion. I firmly believe that this alignment between government vision and institutional mission has not only strengthened SGPGIMS but also advanced the collective goal of ensuring world-class, affordable, and accessible healthcare for every Indian."

28

Revisiting India's Strategic Behaviour @75

Prof. (Dr.) Raj Kumar Kothari[1]

India's strategic behaviour is rooted in its civilisational history which reflects a blend of moral philosophy, pragmatic statecraft, and enduring resilience. India's pursuit of power is, on the one hand, premised on diplomatic manoeuvring and strategic autonomy; and on the other, civilisational ethos that emphasises justice, compassion, and fairness.

At the end of75, a debate cropped up centring around India's material strength vis-à-vis the rest of South Asian states. One school argues that it easily overshadows all other South Asian states. The South Asian states for decades have complained that India acts like a 'big brother', always attempting to impose its will upon others. In support of this narrative, they cite instances of India's intervention in East Pakistan in 1971; dispatch of peacekeeping forces to Sri Lanka in 1987; and the intervention in the Maldives in 1988; India's befitting military response to Pakistan in the wake of Pahalgam terror attack in 2025; and so on.

1. Professor of Political Science, Diamond Harbour Women's University, West Bengal. [Currently serving as the Vice-Chancellor, The Sanskrit College & University, Kolkata]

The second school opines that there are however occasions when the counter narrative that India remained passive or indifferent to different situations which otherwise could have strengthened New Delhi's ability to assert its hegemonic authority. Examples of inaction on the part of India in the potential security threats are plenty. For example, India could have chosen to align with one of the power blocs during the cold war years; New Delhi could have aligned with any big power against China; it could have taken a tougher stand against Pakistan at the Shimla Summit following its victory in 1971; New Delhi did not acquire nuclear weapons when China and Pakistan rapidly moved to acquire the same. Such behaviour challenges the popular neo-realist explanation of India's foreign policy stance. Interestingly, Harsh V Pant opines that there was never a golden age of Indian predominance in South Asia and the Indian Ocean Region. Barry Buzan argues that New Delhi is unable to act in accordance with its actual material strength due to several reasons.

According to many foreign policy scholars, India's foreign policy behaviour fails to match its size and material power. The moot question is why an increasingly powerful India – dominant in all aspects of material capacity – has failed to shape/re-shape the policies and strategic behaviour of South Asian states? This behaviour is even more puzzling in the post-cold war decades when India is arguably more prosperous and militarily more powerful. Analysts like Mariam Prys have sought to explain this disjunction between power and policy by terming it as 'expectation and achievement gap.'

While some scholars trace the gap between expectations to weakness in its domestic economy and politics; others point to the distribution of power beyond India to explain why it is not a hegemonic state. Those who focus on domestic conditions to explain the gap stress that material power need not always translate into military strength, nor will accumulate capabilities make India influential. In Subrata Mitra's view, domestic constraints offer the best reason why India is a 'reluctant hegemon'.

Thus, at the end of seventy-five years of India's independence, we need to address the gap between India's domestic potential and its foreign policy behaviour, keeping in mind the goal of VIKSIT BHARAT by 2047.

29

Transformative Leadership: A Decade of Narendra Modi's Governance

Prof. (Dr.) Rajeev Bhardwaj[1]

The last eleven years of Prime Minister Narendra Modi's leader-ship mark a transformative phase in India's political, economic, and socio-cultural landscape. His governance has not only redefined policy-making but also reshaped the aspirations of over a billion citizens. As someone who has closely observed these years of governance, I find that this journey is characterised by vision, execution, and a renewed sense of national pride.

One of the most remarkable aspects of the Modi era has been his emphasis on *inclusive development*. The slogan *"Sabka Saath, Sabka Vikas, Sabka Vishwas"* has moved beyond rhetoric to become a governing principle. The expansion of welfare schemes such as *Jan Dhan Yojana* for financial inclusion, *Ujjwala Yojana* for providing clean cooking fuel, and *Ayushman Bharat* for universal health coverage, reflect an unprecedented focus on reaching the last mile. These initiatives have brought millions of marginalised citizens into the mainstream of development, creating a more empowered and self-reliant society.

Equally significant has been the government's push towards infrastructure and digital transformation. Under the *Digital India* initiative, internet penetration has surged, bridging the

1. Pro Vice Chancellor, DBS Global University, Dehradun.

urban-rural divide and enabling access to digital governance, education, and entrepreneurship. Roads, highways, airports, and railway modernisation have accelerated, laying the foundation for India's emergence as a global economic power. The vision of *Smart Cities* and emphasis on renewable energy highlight a balanced approach between modernisation and sustainability.

The Modi government has also shown remarkable resilience in dealing with global challenges. During the COVID-19 pandemic, India not only managed one of the world's largest vaccinations drives but also emerged as the "pharmacy of the world" by supplying vaccines to other nations. This reflected both the strength of India's health infrastructure under his leadership and the spirit of *Vasudhaiva Kutumbakam* (the world is one family).

On the international stage, Prime Minister Modi has significantly elevated India's stature. His active diplomacy, from forging strong ties with major powers to strengthening South-South cooperation, has positioned India as a responsible global player. Whether it was advocating for climate justice at global forums or leading the *International Solar Alliance*, Modi's leadership has underscored India's role as both a regional stabilizer and a global leader.

The past eleven years have also been marked by bold reforms in governance. The implementation of GST streamlined indirect taxation across states, while the push for *Atmanirbhar Bharat* (self-reliant India) has encouraged indigenous manufacturing and innovation. Efforts to reform labour laws, agricultural policies, and administrative frameworks reflect the government's commitment to modernisation, even amidst debate and opposition.

Culturally, Modi's governance has reignited a spirit of civilisational pride. Through initiatives like *Kashi Vishwanath Corridor*, promotion of yoga and Ayurveda, and emphasis on India's heritage, the government has sought to connect development with cultural rootedness. This blending of tradition with modernity has created a distinctive model of governance, one that is uniquely Indian yet globally relevant.

While no administration is without its challenges, the Modi government's defining achievement lies in instilling a collective belief that India's time has come. By nurturing confidence among citizens, engaging the diaspora, and presenting India's story of growth with conviction, Modi has ushered in a new narrative of national destiny.

As India stands at the threshold of new opportunities, the past eleven years offer not just a record of governance but a roadmap of aspirations fulfilled and possibilities ahead. Narendra Modi's leadership has, in essence, redefined the grammar of governance, where vision, execution, and accountability converge to build a stronger, confident, and self-reliant India.

30

Opening New Windows to Knowledge Access in India during the Last 11 Years

Dr. Rajeev Manhas and Pratibha

Abstract

In the rapidly evolving information society, accessibility to quality knowledge resources has become the foundation for intellectual growth, social empowerment, and national development. Over the last eleven years, India has witnessed a transformative journey in democratizing access to information, marked by policies, digital infrastructure expansion, and innovations in library and information services. This chapter explores how the nation, once historically known for its restricted access to knowledge during the ancient and medieval periods—where libraries were often confined to royal courts and elite classes—has transitioned into an era where information accessibility is considered a fundamental right. In an age dominated by misinformation, disinformation, and fake narratives, ensuring quality information for citizens is not only a challenge but also an imperative for India's progress in education, health, research, and governance. The chapter outlines the trajectory of knowledge accessibility initiatives in India during the last decade, highlighting government programmes, institutional reforms, technological interventions, and the evolving role of libraries in bridging the digital and knowledge divide.

Introduction

Access to knowledge has historically shaped civilisations, influencing culture, science, and governance. In ancient India, knowledge was preserved through oral traditions and manuscripts, often limited to specific social groups. Libraries, where they existed, were seen as symbols of power and prestige. They were maintained largely by kings and aristocrats, who considered knowledge a royal possession. For centuries, this restricted access created barriers between the learned elite and the common people.

In the modern world, however, information is no longer a luxury for a few; it is a necessity for all. Knowledge is the cornerstone of democracy, innovation, and socio-economic growth. With the exponential rise of misinformation in the digital age, reliable and quality information access has become a matter of national priority. India, or Bharat, stands at a critical juncture in ensuring that every citizen, regardless of geography or socio-economic status, is empowered through equitable access to authentic knowledge.

The last eleven years (2014–2025) have been a period of significant change for India in terms of knowledge accessibility. This era has seen the rise of Digital India, the spread of broadband and mobile internet, the integration of e-governance platforms, and the emergence of national-level digital repositories such as the National Digital Library of India (NDLI), e-ShodhSindhu, and SWAYAM. Libraries have redefined themselves as knowledge hubs rather than silent repositories, embracing technology to remain relevant in an age where information is abundant but authenticity is often questionable.

At the same time, India has faced the challenge of curbing misinformation while enhancing information literacy. Initiatives in health communication during the COVID-19 pandemic, for example, highlighted the urgent need for reliable, timely, and accessible knowledge. Similarly, the academic and research community has benefitted from open access policies, institutional digital repositories, and collaborative platforms that reduce dependency on expensive foreign publishers.

This chapter analyzes how India has opened new windows to knowledge access over the past decade, balancing its rich heritage of scholarship with the demands of the information age. By reflecting on policy measures, technological innovations, and the changing role of libraries, it demonstrates that quality information access is not merely a support system but the very backbone of a nation's progress in today's interconnected world.

1. Historical Context of Knowledge Access in India

Knowledge and information access in India has always been deeply linked to the cultural and political structures of its time. In the ancient period, the **oral tradition** was the dominant mode of transmitting knowledge. The Vedas, Upanishads, and other scriptures were memorised and recited by generations of scholars, but access was often restricted to specific groups within society. The gurukul system of education further reinforced selective access, as learning was limited to those who could afford patronage or belonged to privileged communities.

With the establishment of renowned learning centers such as **Takshashila, Nalanda, and Vikramshila**, India became a global hub of higher education, attracting students and scholars from across Asia. These institutions housed vast collections of manuscripts, functioning as libraries in the classical sense. However, their access remained largely confined to monastic or scholarly elites.

During medieval times, the tradition of royal and court libraries flourished. Kings and emperors commissioned grand collections of manuscripts, particularly in Persian, Sanskrit, and Arabic. Libraries like those of the Mughal emperors, and earlier under Ashoka's patronage, symbolised prestige and intellectual power. Yet, such collections were not public in nature—they served rulers, aristocrats, and religious authorities, not the general population.

The colonial period marked a major turning point. The British administration introduced **public libraries** and academic institutions modeled on European systems. The 19th and early 20th centuries saw the establishment of libraries in Calcutta, Bombay, Madras, and other cities, gradually creating a culture of wider access. However, rural areas remained excluded, and libraries often reflected colonial priorities rather than indigenous needs.

Thus, the history of knowledge access in India reflects a journey from exclusivity to gradual democratization. This background provides context for understanding the radical changes of the last eleven years, where the focus has shifted toward universal, digital, and equitable access to information.

2. The Contemporary Information Landscape and Challenges

In the 21st century, information has become both abundant and contested. India faces the dual challenge of ensuring broad access to knowledge while also safeguarding against misinformation. The **information explosion** through digital platforms has empowered citizens but also created vulnerability to fake news, conspiracy theories, and distorted narratives (Mukherjee, 2020).

The **digital divide** continues to affect equitable access. Urban populations benefit more readily from digital resources, while rural and marginalised communities face limitations due to poor connectivity, lack of digital literacy, and affordability barriers (World Bank, 2023).

At the same time, the growing recognition of **information literacy** has placed libraries, educational institutions, and policy-makers at the center of efforts to ensure that citizens are equipped not only to access information but also to critically evaluate it.

3. Policy Initiatives in India (2014–2025)

The last decade has been crucial in redefining knowledge access in India. A series of national policies and programmes have opened new digital avenues for learners, researchers, and citizens. Key initiatives include:

3.1 Digital India Programme (2015)

Launched by the Government of India, **Digital India** aims to transform the country into a digitally empowered society and knowledge economy. It emphasizes universal digital literacy, broadband highways, e-governance, and electronic delivery of services. Public access points such as Common Service Centres (CSCs) and rural broadband under BharatNet have significantly expanded access to online knowledge resources, even in remote areas (Government of India, 2015).

3.2 National Digital Library of India (NDLI)

Initiated by the Ministry of Education and developed by IIT Kharagpur, the **NDLI** is a pioneering initiative that provides access to over **80 million resources** including books, theses, research articles, and educational videos in multiple languages. It functions as a single-window platform, bridging the gap between learners and global scholarly content (NDLI, 2024).

3.3 SWAYAM and SWAYAM Prabha

The **SWAYAM platform**, launched in 2017, delivers Massive Open Online Courses (MOOCs) across disciplines at no cost to learners. It has democratized higher education by providing quality courses from top institutions like IITs, IIMs, and Central Universities (Ministry of Education, 2017).

Complementing it, **SWAYAM Prabha** uses 34 DTH TV channels to broadcast educational content, thereby reaching students in areas with limited internet connectivity.

3.4 e-ShodhSindhu Consortium

Managed by INFLIBNET, the **e-ShodhSindhu** consortium provides access to thousands of high-quality e-journals, databases, and e-books for Indian universities and research institutions. This initiative reduces dependence on expensive international subscriptions and ensures equitable access for researchers (UGC, 2017).

3.5 National Virtual Library of India (NVLI)

The **NVLI project**, developed by IIT Bombay, aims to create a unified digital repository of India's cultural heritage, manuscripts, and knowledge resources. This initiative supports not just academia but also the preservation and dissemination of India's civilisational knowledge.

3.6 Open Access Policies

Recognizing the importance of free and open dissemination of research, agencies such as the **University Grants Commission** (**UGC**) and **Council of Scientific and Industrial Research** (**CSIR**) have adopted open access mandates. These policies require that publicly funded research be deposited in institutional repositories, thereby enhancing visibility and accessibility of Indian scholarship (CSIR, 2019; Raman, 2022).

3.7 Role During COVID-19 Pandemic

The pandemic accelerated the adoption of digital platforms for learning and research. NDLI, SWAYAM, and institutional repositories played a central role in ensuring continuity of education. Libraries organized online workshops on information literacy and promoted authenticated health resources to counter misinformation (Mehta & Bhattacharya, 2021).

3.8 One Nation One Subscription (ONOS)

On the auspicious occasion of 15 August 2022, PM Modi gave the call of "Jai Anusandhan" (Times of India, 2022). To fulfill his dream and the vision of making India Atmanirbhar and Vikshitbharat@2047, Union Cabinet approved the One Nation One Subscription scheme in 2024. Budget of around ₹ 6,000 crore for 2025–2027 has been allocated for the mission to provide nationwide free access to journals and academic databases through centralized institutional subscriptions. It covers nearly 30 national and international publishers providing access to over 13,000 full-text journals (INFLIBNET, 2025).

3.9 Strengthening INFLIBNET and Library Infrastructure

The Information and Library Network Centre (INFLIBNET) has been the main source of library automation and e-resources in India. During this time, LIS Academy's services, like N-LIST (for e-journals and e-books), Shodhganga (a place to store theses), IndCat (a union catalog), and SOUL (library management software), improved significantly (Library and Information Science Academy, 2024).

Shri Amit Shah, the Union Home Minister, went to the INFLIBNET Center in Gandhinagar in 2024 and stressed the need to make digital services available to everyone. He also launched the Sastu Sahitya Vardhak Karyalay mobile app, aimed at promoting affordable digital reading (Times of India, 2025).

3.10 Preservation of Ancient Knowledge

The Modi government has additionally made important contributions to the digitization of culture. The organizations like Indira Gandhi National Centre for the Arts (IGNCA) organizations started projects like the Vedic Heritage Portal and the virtual museum Kala Vaibhav to digitally preserve manuscripts, ancient texts, and cultural artifacts. The recently announced "Gyan Bharatam Mission," will also digitize rare manuscripts and create a National Digital Repository. This will make sure that India's ancient knowledge and traditions have global outreach (Outlook India, 2024).

3.11 Reading Culture and the Festival of Libraries

The Festival of Libraries 2023 was held in New Delhi to create enthusiasm for reading among young people. Prime Minister Modi said that improving library infrastructure and encouraging creative writing are important steps toward creating a culture of lifelong learning. The event also brought together historic places like the Rampur Raza Library and the Khuda Baksh Library, showing how important they are in a digital age (Press Information Bureau, 2023).

4. Technological Transformations in Libraries

The last eleven years have seen a paradigm shift in how libraries function in India. Traditional libraries, once confined to physical collections, have adopted hybrid and digital models to stay relevant in an era of ubiquitous information. This transformation has been accelerated by the availability of affordable internet, cloud computing, and mobile technologies (Kaur & Verma, 2018).

Institutional repositories have emerged as powerful tools for archiving and disseminating research outputs. Many universities and research organisations now maintain digital repositories aligned with **Open Access (OA)** mandates. Similarly, platforms like **Krishikosh** (agriculture) and **Shodhganga** (theses and dissertations) have made subject-specific knowledge more accessible.

Artificial Intelligence (AI) and machine learning have also begun to influence library services, such as automated cataloguing, personalised recommendation systems, and chatbots for reference services (Sahoo & Mohanty, 2021). QR codes, library mobile applications, and virtual reality-based learning spaces are further enhancing user engagement.

These innovations underscore the transformation of libraries from passive repositories of books into **interactive knowledge hubs**, enabling seamless access to resources anytime, anywhere.

5. Role of Libraries in Combating Misinformation

In the age of digital abundance, the credibility of information has become as important as accessibility. Misinformation, disinformation, and fake narratives—especially on social media—pose significant challenges for informed decision-making in India (Mukherjee, 2020).

Libraries have positioned themselves as **knowledge guardians** by providing access to curated, peer-reviewed, and authentic information resources. Many academic libraries conducted **information literacy programmes** during the COVID-19 pandemic to guide students and researchers in identifying reliable health information (Mehta & Bhattacharya, 2021).

Furthermore, public libraries have engaged in community outreach programmes, such as digital literacy camps, awareness drives, and fact-checking workshops. By reinforcing critical thinking and research skills, libraries act as frontline institutions against the misinformation epidemic.

6. Inclusivity and Accessibility

A critical dimension of knowledge access in India is inclusivity. While digital initiatives have expanded, bridging the **digital divide** between urban and rural, privileged and marginalised communities remains essential (World Bank, 2023).

Programmes such as **BharatNet** have provided broadband connectivity to rural areas, enabling villagers to access educational resources and e-governance services. For the differently abled, platforms like **Sugamya Pustakalaya**, an online accessible library for persons with print disabilities, have opened new possibilities (DAISY India, 2022).

Multilingual knowledge dissemination is another crucial step. NDLI and NVLI provide resources in multiple Indian languages, ensuring that linguistic diversity does not remain a barrier to knowledge access. Moreover, initiatives like SWAYAM Prabha, which broadcasts educational content via satellite television, ensure that even those without internet connectivity can access quality learning materials.

This shift from exclusivity to inclusivity demonstrates India's commitment to making knowledge a **fundamental right** for every citizen, irrespective of geography, socio-economic status, or ability.

7. Future Directions for Knowledge Accessibility in India

As India advances toward becoming a **knowledge economy,** several future directions are evident. First, the integration of **AI-driven knowledge systems** can enhance personalisation, data analytics, and predictive information services. Second, stronger collaborations between academia, government, and industry are required to sustain innovations in digital learning and open access publishing (Raman, 2022).

Expandingopenaccesspublishingin Indiawillreducereliance on costly foreign publishers, while also enhancing the global visibility of Indian research. Additionally, developing **citizen-**

centric knowledge ecosystems—where libraries, schools, NGOs, and digital platforms work together—can deepen the culture of lifelong learning.

The focus must shift from mere "information access" to **knowledge empowerment**, where users are equipped not only to retrieve information but also to evaluate, apply, and generate new knowledge. This vision aligns with the aspirations of the **National Education Policy 2020 (NEP 2020)**, which emphasizes technology-enabled, equitable, and inclusive access to education (Ministry of Education, 2020).

8. Conclusion

India's journey of knowledge access reflects a remarkable transformation. From the exclusivity of ancient royal libraries and scholarly institutions, the country has moved to a **democratized, digital, and inclusive knowledge ecosystem**. Over the past eleven years, initiatives such as Digital India, NDLI, SWAYAM, and e-Shodh Sindhu have opened unprecedented windows to information, bridging gaps between privileged and marginalised sections of society.

Yet, challenges persist in combating misinformation and ensuring equitable digital literacy. Libraries are at the forefront of this struggle, evolving as dynamic institutions that combine heritage with innovation.

In a world where information shapes democracy, economy, and culture, India's progress in ensuring **quality information accessibility** reaffirms that knowledge is not just a developmental input but the very foundation of nation-building. Sustained investments in digital infrastructure, open access, and information literacy will ensure that India continues to lead in the global knowledge society.

References

- Council of Scientific and Industrial Research. (2019). *Open access policy of CSIR*. Government of India.
- DAISY India. (2022). *Sugamya Pustakalaya: Accessible online library.* https://library.daisyindia.org
- Government of India. (2015). *Digital India: Power to empower.* Ministry of Electronics and Information Technology.
- INFLIBNET. (2025). *One Nation One Subscription: An initiative of Government of India.* https://www.onos.gov.in/
- Kaur, H., & Verma, R. (2018). Digital transformation of libraries in India: Challenges and opportunities. *Journal of Library and Information Technology*, 38(5), 327–334.
- Library and Information Science Academy. (2024). *The Growth and Future of Information Institutions in India.* https://lis.academy/library-information-and-society/growth-future-information-institutions-india/
- Mehta, P., & Bhattacharya, S. (2021). Information literacy in times of pandemic: Role of Indian libraries. *Annals of Library and Information Studies*, 68(2), 121–128.
- Ministry of Education. (2017). *SWAYAM: Study webs of active learning for young aspiring minds*. Government of India. https://swayam.gov.in
- Ministry of Education. (2020). *National Education Policy 2020.* Government of India.
- Mukherjee, A. (2020). Information disorder in India: Challenges of misinformation and fake news. *Media Watch*, 11(2), 246–259.
- National Digital Library of India. (2024). *NDLI resources and services.* https://ndl.iitkgp.ac.in
- Outlook India. (2024). *Modi Govt Securing Knowledge of India's Ancient Books, Manuscripts Through Technology: Shah.* https://www.outlook india.com/national/modi-govt-securing-knowledge-of-india-s-ancient-books-manuscripts-through-technology-shah-news-272555
- Press Information Bureau. (2023). *Emphasis on improving infrastructure in our libraries will spread awareness on the importance of reading: Prime Minister.* https://www.pib.gov.in/PressReleasePage.aspx?PRID=1946220

- Raman, A. (2022). Open access and India's research future. *Current Science*, 122(10), 1135–1138.
- Sahoo, J., & Mohanty, S. (2021). Artificial intelligence applications in libraries: An Indian perspective. *Library Philosophy and Practice*, 2021, 1–12.
- Times of India. (2022). Jai Anusandhan: *PM Modi gives 'Jai Anusandhan' slogan to push for innovation.* https://timesofindia.indiatimes.com/india/pm-modi-gives-jai-anusandhan-slogan-to-push-for-innovation/articleshow/93570 446.cms.
- Times of India. (2025). *Amit Shah visits INFLIBNET centre in Gandhinagar.* https://timesofindia.indiatimes.com/city/ahmedabad/amit-shah-visits-inflibnet-centre-in-gandhinagar/articleshow/122119004.cmsUniversity Grants Commission. (2017). *e-ShodhSindhu: Consortium for higher education e-resources.* INFLIBNET Centre. https://ess.inflibnet. ac.in
- University Grants Commission. (2017). *e-ShodhSindhu: Consortium for higher education e-resources.* INFLIBNET Centre. https://ess.inflibnet.ac.in
- World Bank. (2023). *Digital development in South Asia: India's progress.* Washington, DC: World Bank.

31

Eleven Years of Governance and Growth: An academic perspective from Gujarat

Prof. (Dr.) Rajul K. Gajjar[1]

Over the past eleven years, under the leadership of Prime Minister Shri Narendra Modi, India has undergone a remarkable transformation. As an academic leader of a state university in Gujarat—a region shaped by Shri Modi's political vision—I have had the opportunity to observe this national transformation, both in terms of broader policy changes and their impact at the local level. The changes are not just statistical or policy-driven; they have touched institutions, communities, and individual lives.

The Prime Minister's emphasis on efficient governance, infrastructure, and innovation has had a profound impact on Gujarat. The GIFT City project, India's first International Financial Services Centre, located in Gandhinagar, reflects the shift from traditional economic hubs to futuristic, globally integrated ecosystems. It is no coincidence that Gujarat is now seen not just as an industrial powerhouse but as a hub for financial, digital, and educational innovation.

1. Vice Chancellor, Gujarat Technological University.

The Digital India initiative has brought measurable improvements in the way universities like ours function. Student admissions, scholarship disbursements, examination systems, and even academic audits are now seamlessly conducted through robust digital platforms. The Aadhaar-enabled Direct Benefit Transfer (DBT) mechanism has made financial support schemes more accessible and transparent. I have personally witnessed the confidence this builds in students from marginalised communities, as they no longer have to navigate bureaucratic inefficiencies to receive what is rightfully theirs (UIDAI, 2023).

Another transformative initiative that has left a noticeable imprint on higher education and youth innovation is the Start-up India Mission. Since its launch in 2016, the programme has catalyzed a vibrant start-up ecosystem, particularly among engineering and management students across Gujarat (DPIIT, 2024). At Gujarat Technological University, we have seen a surge in student-led start-ups nurtured through institutional incubation centres, hackathons, and government-accredited innovation councils. The establishment of the Student Start-up and Innovation Policy (SSIP) by the Government of Gujarat, in alignment with the national vision, has empowered thousands of students to convert their ideas into viable enterprises (Government of Gujarat, 2022). It is encouraging to witness young minds engaging not just in placement-oriented learning, but in entrepreneurship that addresses local problems with scalable, technology-driven solutions. This shift from job-seeking to job-creating reflects a deeper cultural transformation in our academic campuses—one that is supported by government policy, industry linkage, and faculty mentorship.

India's semiconductor revolution is progressing in mission mode with ₹1.5 trillion investment support and 50% financial assistance from the Government of India. As Hon'ble PM Shri Narendra Modi rightly stated, *"Our dream is that every device in the world will have an Indian-made chip"* (PIB, 2024). This vision drives India's path toward technological self-reliance and global leadership. Gujarat, being at the forefront with world-class semiconductor manufacturing facilities, holds a pivotal role in this journey. Anticipating future workforce needs, GTU has introduced dedicated degree programmes, Centres of Excellence, and industry-linked courses to skill students and faculty for this sunrise sector.

One of the major initiatives that holds significant relevance for the academic community is the National Education Policy (NEP) 2020. Its focus on promoting regional languages, skill-based learning, and multidisciplinary education is well-aligned with the cultural and linguistic diversity of Gujarat. At GTU, efforts are underway for the implementation of the thrust areas of NEP 2020 into our curricula. Such initiatives not only enrich the academic content but also make learning more rooted in the socio-cultural realities of our students. This approach reflects not merely the implementation of policy mandates, but a deeper process of institutional adaptation and internalisation of the NEP's vision.

According to the Economic Survey 2024, rural sanitation coverage has significantly improved under the Swachh Bharat Mission (Government of India, 2024). A large number of villages in Gujarat have moved from opendefecation-free status to the more advanced ODFPlus level, ensuring proper waste management and hygiene. These changes are not abstract—they have reshaped rural health landscapes in Gujarat's villages. Meanwhile, evidence suggests that access to clean fuel under Ujjwala Yojana has contributed to improved school attendance among girls (Patra & Singh, 2021). As an educator, it is heartening to see how these improvements contribute indirectly to student attendance, especially among female learners.

The Jal Jeevan Mission, which has ensured tap water connections in over 14 crore rural households nationwide

(Ministry of Jal Shakti, 2025), has seen remarkable success in Saurashtra and Kutch—regions long affected by water scarcity. It is in these places that policy becomes personal, and governance becomes transformative.

Gujarat has also been central to symbolic national projects such as the Statue of Unity, which not only honors the legacy of Shri Sardar Vallabhbhai Patel but also instils a sense of unity and pride among students who visit it as part of civic education programmes. Its tourism impact has created jobs, boosted local infrastructure, and reaffirmed the cultural identity of the region.

Being an academic leader in this decade of change has been both humbling and inspiring. The Modi government's focus on capacity-building, digital governance, and inclusive development aligns closely with the evolving role of universities—not merely as knowledge providers, but as institutions of transformation. Our mandate has expanded from academic excellence to social responsibility.

Ensuring equity in the digital divide and balancing autonomy with accountability—the vision of a Viksit Bharat (Developed India) by 2047 is within reach. Gujarat's story, and GTU's journey as an institution, affirm that we are not just observing history—we are participating in its making.

References

- Department for Promotion of Industry and Internal Trade (DPIIT). (2024). *Start-up India Annual Report 2023–24*. Ministry of Commerce and Industry, Government of India. Retrieved from https://www.startupindia.gov.in
- Government of Gujarat. (2022). *Student Start-up and Innovation Policy (SSIP) – Progress Report*. Gujarat Knowledge Society. Retrieved from https://www.ssipgujarat.in
- Government of India. (2024). *Economic Survey 2023–24*. Ministry of Finance. Retrieved from https://www.indiabudget.gov.in/economicsurvey/

- Ministry of Housing and Urban Affairs (MoHUA). (2021). *Swachh Bharat Mission – Urban: Progress report*. Government of India. Retrieved from https://swachhbharaturban.gov.in
- Ministry of Jal Shakti. (2025). *Jal Jeevan Mission Dashboard*. Government of India. Retrieved from https://ejalshakti.gov.in/jjmreport/
- Patra, A., & Singh, N. (2021). *Access to clean cooking fuel and girls' schooling outcomes in India*. arXiv. https://arxiv.org/abs/2106.01815
- Press Information Bureau (PIB). (2024). *PM's address on India's semiconductor mission*. Government of India. Retrieved from https://pib.gov.in

32

India on the Rise: Reflections on 11 Years of Transformative Governance under Prime Minister Narendra Modi

Prof. Santosh Kumar Tripathy[1]

The past eleven years have witnessed a remarkable transformation in India's developmental landscape under the leadership of Prime Minister Narendra Modi. From significant policy reforms to targeted welfare interventions, India has undergone a silent revolution in its economic, social, and global standing. As an academic and administrator closely observing and participating in India's higher education and research ecosystem, I have seen first-hand how this transformation has positively impacted institutions, aspirations, and ambitions alike.

One of the most defining features of Prime Minister Modi's governance has been the clarity of vision and strength of purpose. The idea of "Sabka Saath, Sabka Vikas, Sabka Vishwas, Sabka Prayas" has not only shaped the discourse on inclusive development but has translated into actionable policies across sectors. Flagship initiatives like Digital India, Make in India, Startup India, and Skill India have empowered the youth and

1. Vice-Chancellor, Fakir Mohan University, Vyasa, Balasore-20, Odisha (India).

laid the foundation for a knowledge-driven economy. These schemes are no longer just slogans - they are enabling lakhs of young Indians to innovate, create, and contribute.

Infrastructure development has also seen unprecedented momentum. Whether it is the construction of highways, the expansion of railway networks, or the thrust on renewable energy, the Modi government's emphasis on connectivity and sustainability has been consistent and far-reaching. The Ujjwala Yojana, rural electrification, housing for all, and Har Ghar Jal Mission have elevated the standard of living for millions, especially in rural and marginalised communities.

In higher education and research, we have experienced both structural reforms and increased investment. The National Education Policy (NEP) 2020 stands as a landmark achievement, aiming to decolonize the mind-set of Indian education and align it with future-readiness and global relevance. The emphasis on multidisciplinary education, vocational training, research innovation, and international collaboration has already started yielding positive outcomes. Institutions are being encouraged to become globally competitive, while also being deeply rooted in Indian values and knowledge systems.

India's emergence on the global stage has been equally significant. Prime Minister Modi's proactive diplomacy and strategic foreign engagements have enhanced India's stature as a responsible and influential global player. Be it leadership in climate negotiations, the bold handling of cross-border challenges, or the promotion of international yoga and cultural diplomacy India is today viewed as a confident, self-reliant, and forward-looking nation. The success of the G20 presidency under India and the launch of platforms like the International Solar Alliance further testify to India's growing global footprint.

It is also important to acknowledge that global technological advancements, increased digital penetration, and greater interconnectivity during this period have complemented India's development story. The momentum of global innovation, the rise of AI, big data, and emerging technologies, as well as cross-border collaborations, have created a conducive environment that the Modi government has leveraged with great effectiveness.

As a Vice-Chancellor, I have observed how policy consistency, digital empowerment, and mission-mode implementation at the national level have trickled down to universities and research institutions. From increased funding support to digitization of academic processes and encouragement for industry-academia linkages - the changes are visible and tangible.

In conclusion, the 11 years of Prime Minister Narendra Modi's leadership reflect a paradigm shift in governance marked by inclusivity, innovation, and internationalism. India is no longer content being a developing country - it is aspiring and preparing to lead. This journey of transformation is still unfolding, but the foundations laid during this decade will guide the nation for generations to come.

33

Manipur: The Powerhouse of Indian Sports and the Vision of National Sports University

Dr. Shyam Sundar Rath[1]

Manipur has rightfully earned the title of the *"Powerhouse of Sports in India"* for its exceptional contributions to the nation's sporting excellence. This small northeastern state has consistently produced world-class athletes who have brought glory to India on global platforms, including the Olympics, Asian Games, and World Championships. With an impressive tally of 19 Olympians excelling in disciplines such as hockey, weightlifting, boxing, judo, and archery, Manipur's sporting legacy stands unmatched. The achievements of its athletes, many of whom have secured medals at the highest levels, have reinforced India's growing prominence in the global sports arena.

Recognizing Manipur's pivotal role in shaping India's sports culture, Prime Minister Narendra Modi, in a historic and visionary step, initiated the establishment of the National Sports University (NSU)—the first of its kind in India. The foundation stone was laid by the Prime Minister himself on March 16, 2018, and the university was formally brought into

1. Vice-Chancellor (O), National Sports University, Manipur.

existence through an Act of Parliament the same year. This landmark decision reflects the Modi-led BJP government's steadfast commitment to nurturing future champions through world-class infrastructure, research, and education.

A National Hub for Sports Excellence

NSU is envisioned as a premier institution advancing sports education in specialised fields such as Sports Science, Sports Technology, Sports Management, and Sports Coaching. It also functions as a National Training Centre for select sports disciplines, integrating international best practices to enhance India's competitive edge. While the permanent campus at Koutruk, Imphal West, is under construction, the university is already operational from its temporary campus at Khuman Lampak Sports Complex, attracting talented students from across the country who are pursuing advanced sports education.

Early Impact and National Recognition

Even in its early years, NSU has shown remarkable results. Its students and alumni have excelled in inter-university, national, and international events, bringing laurels to the institution. Significantly, NSU alumni contributed as Sports Psychologists to the Indian Shooting team at the Paris Olympics 2024, exemplifying the university's multidisciplinary approach and its ability to contribute to high-performance sport in diverse ways.

Part of a Larger Vision

The creation of NSU is in perfect alignment with Prime Minister Modi's larger vision of transforming India into a global sporting powerhouse. Under his leadership, sports has been elevated to a national priority, with landmark initiatives such as Khelo India, Target Olympic Podium Scheme (TOPS), expansion of rural sports infrastructure, and targeted athlete support schemes. The Modi-led BJP government has focused not only on elite athletes but also on grassroots development, women's participation in sports, and integrating sports science into training systems nationwide.

For Manipur, these efforts have translated into modern training facilities, greater international exposure for athletes, and a renewed sense of pride as a model for sports-driven growth.

Conclusion

The National Sports University stands as a living testament to how visionary governance can transform a state's natural strengths into national assets. By placing this prestigious institution in Manipur—a land with an unyielding sporting spirit—the Modi government has both honored the region's legacy and laid the foundation for a new era of Indian sporting dominance. As NSU continues to grow, it will play a decisive role in fulfilling the Prime Minister's inspiring call: *"Khelega India, Toh Khilega India."*

This milestone is not merely an institutional achievement—it is part of the enduring legacy of 11 years of the Modi Government, a period that has redefined India's sports ecosystem and empowered the youth to dream, strive, and achieve on the world stage.

Prof. SOM NATH
VICE-CHANCELLOR
Ph.D (Civil Engineering), ME (Highways)
MIRC, MIUT, MISTE, MISRMTT

प्रो० सोमनाथ
कुलपति

Kurukshetra University,
Kurukshetra - 136 119 (INDIA)
(Established by the State Legislature Act XII of 1956)
(A++ Grade, NAAC Accredited)

कुरुक्षेत्र विश्वविद्यालय,
कुरुक्षेत्र - 136 119 (भारत)
(राज्य विधान सभा के एक्ट XII द्वारा 1956 से स्थापित)
(A++ ग्रेड, नैक प्रत्यायित)

माननीय प्रधानमंत्री श्री नरेंद्र मोदी जी के नेतृत्व में केंद्र सरकार द्वारा शिक्षा, युवा सशक्तिकरण, रोजगार और स्वदेशी के साथ–साथ अन्य क्षेत्रों में की गई अविस्मरणीय सुधारात्मक पहल

माननीय प्रधानमंत्री श्री नरेंद्र मोदी जी के नेतृत्व में भारत ने शिक्षा, युवा सशक्तिकरण, रोजगार और स्वदेशी के क्षेत्र में अभूतपूर्व प्रगति की है। उनकी दूरदर्शी नीतियों और योजनाओं ने देश को एक समावेशी, आत्मनिर्भर और वैश्विक स्तर पर सशक्त राष्ट्र के रूप में स्थापित किया है। इन पहलों ने न केवल आर्थिक और सामाजिक विकास को गति दी है, बल्कि भारत की सांस्कृतिक और राष्ट्रीय पहचान को भी मजबूती प्रदान की है।

राष्ट्रीय शिक्षा नीति (एनईपी) 2020 ने भारतीय शिक्षा प्रणाली में क्रांतिकारी बदलाव लाया है। यह नीति बहु–विषयक शिक्षा, कौशल विकास और अनुसंधान को बढ़ावा देने पर केंद्रित है, जिससे शिक्षा समग्र, समावेशी और रोजगार–उन्मुख बनी है। डिजिटल इंडिया पहल के तहत स्वयं (SWAYAM) और एनपीटीईएल जैसे ऑनलाइन मंचों ने शिक्षा को ग्रामीण और दूरस्थ क्षेत्रों तक पहुंचाया है। ये मंच उच्च गुणवत्ता वाली शिक्षा प्रदान करते हैं, जिससे युवा अपनी शिक्षा को ऑनलाइन माध्यम से आगे बढ़ा सकते हैं और रोजगार के अवसरों तक पहुंच सकते हैं।

स्किल इंडिया मिशन ने युवाओं को तकनीकी और व्यावसायिक कौशल प्रदान करके उनकी रोजगार क्षमता में वृद्धि की है। यह मिशन युवाओं को आत्मनिर्भर बनाने और उद्योगों की मांग के अनुरूप तैयार करने में महत्वपूर्ण भूमिका निभा रहा है। स्टार्टअप इंडिया योजना ने उद्यमिता को प्रोत्साहन दिया है, जिसमें युवाओं को नवाचार, वित्तीय सहायता, मेंटरशिप और संसाधनों के माध्यम से स्वरोजगार के अवसर प्रदान किए गए हैं। प्रधानमंत्री रोजगार सृजन कार्यक्रम ने ग्रामीण और शहरी क्षेत्रों में सूक्ष्म और लघु उद्योगों को बढ़ावा देकर रोजगार सृजन को गति दी है, जिससे स्थानीय अर्थव्यवस्था को मजबूती मिली है।

माननीय प्रधानमंत्री श्री नरेन्द्र मोदी जी के आह्वान पर आत्मनिर्भर भारत अभियान और वोकल फॉर लोकल पहल ने स्वदेशी उत्पादों और कारीगरों को प्राथमिकता देकर स्थानीय उद्योगों को बल प्रदान किया है। इन पहलों ने वैश्विक बाजार में भारतीय उत्पादों की मांग बढ़ाई है और स्थानीय अर्थव्यवस्था को सशक्त बनाया है। मेक इन इंडिया कार्यक्रम ने औद्योगिक विकास को प्रोत्साहित किया है, जिससे रोजगार सृजन और आर्थिक आत्मनिर्भरता में वृद्धि हुई है।

प्रधानमंत्री ग्राम सड़क योजना ने ग्रामीण क्षेत्रों को शहरी केंद्रों से जोड़कर बुनियादी ढांचे के विकास को गति दी है। स्वच्छ भारत अभियान ने स्वच्छता को राष्ट्रीय प्राथमिकता बनाया, जिससे सार्वजनिक स्वास्थ्य में सुधार हुआ है। आयुष्मान भारत योजना ने गरीब और मध्यम वर्ग के परिवारों को किफायती स्वास्थ्य सेवाएं प्रदान की हैं। उज्ज्वला योजना ने ग्रामीण परिवारों को स्वच्छ ईंधन उपलब्ध कराया, जबकि किसान सम्मान निधि ने कृषि क्षेत्र को आर्थिक सहायता प्रदान की है। जीएसटी (वस्तु एवं सेवा कर) ने भारत को एक एकीकृत बाजार बनाया, जिससे व्यापार और वाणिज्य में सुगमता आई है। यह सब माननीय प्रधानमंत्री श्री नरेन्द्र मोदी जी के कुशल नेतृत्व का ही परिणाम है।

अंतरराष्ट्रीय स्तर पर, मोदी सरकार ने जी–20 शिखर सम्मेलन की अध्यक्षता और जलवायु परिवर्तन पर वैश्विक नेतृत्व के माध्यम से भारत की साख को बढ़ाया है। कोविड–19 महामारी के दौरान, सरकार ने स्वास्थ्य ढांचे को मजबूत किया और विश्व के सबसे बड़े टीकाकरण अभियान को सफलतापूर्वक लागू किया, जिसने लाखों जीवन बचाए और वैश्विक स्वास्थ्य समुदाय में सराहना प्राप्त की। नमामि गंगे परियोजना ने गंगा नदी की स्वच्छता और पारिस्थितिक संतुलन को बहाल करने में महत्वपूर्ण योगदान दिया है।

वैश्विक चुनौतियों के बावजूद माननीय प्रधानमंत्री मोदी जी के नेतृत्व में भारत ने तेज विकास गति बनाए रखी, महंगाई नियंत्रण में रही, और देश ने महामारी जैसे संकटों का सफलतापूर्वक सामना किया।

राष्ट्रीय सुरक्षा के क्षेत्र में भी उल्लेखनीय उपलब्धियाँ दर्ज हुईं हैं। इसी कड़ी में ऑपरेशन सिंदूर की ऐतिहासिक सफलता भारत की सैन्य शक्ति, तकनीकी दक्षता और निर्णायक नेतृत्व का प्रमाण है। प्रधानमंत्री नरेंद्र मोदी जी के नेतृत्व में भारतीय सेना ने इस मिशन को सफल बनाकर देशवासियों में सुरक्षा का भरोसा और दुश्मनों में भय पैदा किया।

कुरुक्षेत्र विश्वविद्यालय ने भी राज्य सरकार के साथ–साथ केंद्र सरकार की नीतियों के साथ पूर्ण संरेखण में शिक्षा, अनुसंधान और बुनियादी ढांचे के क्षेत्र में उल्लेखनीय प्रगति की है। विश्वविद्यालय भारत का पहला विश्वविद्यालय बन गया है, जिसने एनईपी 2020 को अपने परिसर और संबद्ध कॉलेजों में पूरी तरह लागू किया। अगस्त 2022 से स्नातक पाठ्यक्रमों में और 2023 के शैक्षणिक सत्र से संबद्ध कॉलेजों में इस नीति को लागू किया गया। मास्टर ट्रेनर्स के लिए कार्यशालाओं का आयोजन कर नई शिक्षा नीति का प्रभावी कार्यान्वयन सुनिश्चित किया गया। विश्वविद्यालय को हरियाणा के एकमात्र राज्य विश्वविद्यालय के रूप में नैक द्वारा ए–प्लस–प्लस ग्रेड प्रदान किया गया है, जो जनवरी 2031 तक वैध है। पिछले तीन वर्षों में 60–65 पेटेंट दाखिल किए गए, जिनमें से 30 से अधिक स्वीकृत हुए हैं। ये पेटेंट शिक्षा, कृषि, खेल और उद्योग जैसे क्षेत्रों पर केंद्रित हैं। कुरुक्षेत्र विश्वविद्यालय द्वारा राष्ट्रीय और अंतरराष्ट्रीय संस्थानों के साथ 50 से अधिक समझौता ज्ञापनों पर हस्ताक्षर किए गए हैं,

जिससे शैक्षिक और अनुसंधान सहयोग को बढ़ावा मिला है। केजी से पीजी योजना ने प्रारंभिक शिक्षा से स्नातकोत्तर स्तर तक एक सुसंगत शैक्षिक मार्ग प्रदान किया है। नए शैक्षिक और ऑनलाइन कार्यक्रमों ने शिक्षा को सुदूर क्षेत्रों तक पहुंचाया है। विश्वविद्यालय ने अपने बुनियादी ढांचे का व्यापक विकास किया, जिससे छात्रों और खिलाड़ियों की सुविधाएं बेहतर हुई हैं।

(सोमनाथ)

Phone: 01744-238039 (Off.), 238021 (Resi.)
Email: vc@kuk.ac.in

35

11 Years of Modi Government's Achievements in Sports: From Swarnim Gujarat to Olympic Aspirations and Vikshit Bharat 2047

Prof. (Dr.) Sudhir Kumar Sharma[1]

Over the last eleven years, Indian sports have undergone a remarkable transformation under the visionary leadership of Hon'ble Prime Minister Shri Narendrabhai Modi Government. From igniting a culture of grassroots participation to investing in world-class infrastructure, the government's policies have reshaped the nation's sporting landscape. This journey, rooted in the values of excellence, inclusion, and national pride, has strategically progressed toward the ambitious goal of a **Vikshit Bharat (Developed India) by 2047**—with sports as a key driver of social cohesion and global identity.

Foundational Vision: Swarnim Gujarat Sports University (2011)

The story begins in 2011, when Shri Narendra Modi Ji, the then Chief Minister of Gujarat, laid the foundation for the **Swarnim Gujarat Sports University (SGSU)** in Vadodara. This

1. Associate Professor, Department of Physical Education, & Director, Placement Cell, Swarnim Gujarat Sports University, Desar, Vadodara, Gujarat, India.

marked a pioneering step in institutionalising sports education, aiming to produce skilled athletes, coaches, physical educators, and sports administrators. As the first of its kind in the region, SGSU represented a forward-thinking model that integrated academic rigor with athletic excellence. Over the years, it has emerged as a center of excellence, contributing to the national and international sports arena, and serving as a blueprint for similar institutions across India.

Grassroots Revolution: Khel Mahakhumbh and Khelo India

Simultaneously, Gujarat witnessed the launch of **Khel Mahakhumbh**, a state-level sporting movement that encouraged participation across age groups and abilities—including youth, women, the elderly, and persons with disabilities. The inclusive and large-scale nature of this initiative democratized sports and brought it into the daily lives of millions.

Building on this model, the Central Government launched the **Khelo India** programme in 2018, a landmark policy reform that redefined talent identification and athlete support in the country. With the motto ***"Khelo India, Khilao India,"*** the scheme introduced structured athlete scholarships, improved training ecosystems, and facilitated access to international-standard facilities. To date, more than 3,000 young athletes have benefitted from this initiative—many of whom have gone on to represent India in prestigious international competitions. Khelo India has catalyzed the development of sports infrastructure across states, deepened grassroots engagement, and inspired a sporting culture that is both sustainable and inclusive.

Future-Focused Ambition: India's Olympic Dream

Looking ahead, the Modi Government has articulated a bold vision—to host the **2036 Olympic Games.** Efforts are well underway to make this dream a reality, with infrastructural developments like the ***Sardar Vallabhbhai Patel Sports Enclave*** in Ahmedabad positioned as a potential Olympic hub. This endeavour involves robust international collabo-rations, city-level planning, and a strategic bidding approach aligned with global standards.

Beyond infrastructure, the Olympic dream reflects India's aspiration to emerge as a sporting superpower. It underscores the government's belief that sport is not just about medals—it is a symbol of national identity, youth empowerment, and international diplomacy.

Towards Vikshit Bharat 2047: Sports as a Pillar of Development

All these initiatives converge into the broader national vision of **Vikshit Bharat 2047**, which envisions India as a fully developed nation by its centenary of independence. Here, sports are not seen as mere extracurricular activity but as a key pillar of development—linked with health (via the *Fit India Movement*), education (through integration in school and higher curricula), employment (via sports-linked livelihoods), and soft power (through international recognition).

This holistic perspective repositions sports as a catalyst for societal progress—where participation is not limited by gender, geography, or physical ability. Whether through rural talent scouting, specialised training centers, or sports science research, the government is embedding sports into the national development narrative.

Conclusion

The Modi Government's 11-year journey in sports is a story of bold vision, strategic execution, and inclusive growth. From the establishment of Swarnim Gujarat Sports University to the launch of Khelo India, the pursuit of Olympic excellence, and the roadmap to Vikshit Bharat 2047, India is undergoing a sporting renaissance. This renaissance is not just aimed at winning medals, but at fostering a **fitter, prouder, and more united nation**, where sports play a central role in shaping the country's future.

References

1. Government of India. (2018). *Khelo India: National Programme for Development of Sports*. Ministry of Youth Affairs and Sports. https://yas.nic.in/sports/khelo-india
2. Khel Mahakhumbh. (n.d.). *Sports Authority of Gujarat*. https://khelmaha-kumbh.gujarat.gov.in
3. Swarnim Gujarat Sports University. (n.d.). *About SGSU*. https://sgsu.gujarat.gov.in
4. Sharma, S. K. (2024). *11 years of Modi Government's achievements in sports: From Swarnim Gujarat to Olympic aspirations and Vikshit Bharat 2047*. Swarnim Gujarat Sports University. [Unpublished article].
5. Swarnim Gujarat Sports University Act, Government of Gujarat. (2011). *The Swarnim Gujarat Sports University Act, 2011 (Gujarat Act No. 22 of 2011)*. https://sgsu.gujarat.gov.in
6. Press Information Bureau. (2023, December 15). *India's bid for 2036 Olympic Games and sports infrastructure development under Modi Government*. Ministry of Youth Affairs and Sports. https://pib.gov.in
7. Fit India Movement. (n.d.). *Ministry of Youth Affairs and Sports*. https://fitindia.gov.in
8. Sharma, S. K. (n.d.). *Detailed biodata*. Retrieved July 24, 2025, from https://docs.google.com/document/d/1-YiLn4zujZZ3nJ7d2-8nxIcUiytKLPYn/edit

36

Healthcare and Medical Education Transformation under 11 Years of the Modi Government

Prof. (Dr.) Surender Kashyap[1]

Healthcare and Medical Education Transformations under 11 Years of the Modi Government

Healthcare forms the bedrock of human development, while medical education provides the backbone of trained professionals needed to sustain it. Together, they determine the quality of life, productivity, and resilience of a nation. Over the past eleven years, India has undergone a remarkable transformation in both these spheres under the leadership of Prime Minister Shri Narendra Modi. From reducing maternal and infant mortality to creating the world's largest health assurance scheme, and from expanding medical colleges to introducing competency-based curricula, the government has undertaken bold and innovative measures that are steadily bridging long-standing gaps.

This article critically examines the progress achieved in healthcare delivery and medical education between 2014 and 2025, highlighting flagship programmes, quantitative outcomes, and future priorities. It situates India's reforms in a

1. MD (Medicine, PGI), DNB (Resp. Med) FAMS, FCCP, FNCCP, FICS, FICP, AFACA, FSASS, FAPSR, UICC Fellow, Vice Chancellor Atal Medical and Research University, HP Nerchowk, Mandi, Himachal Pradesh - 175008, India.

global context, drawing attention to both achievements and challenges that remain.

1. Strengthening India's Healthcare System

1.1 The Complexity of Indian Healthcare

India's healthcare system is unique in its diversity and complexity. It combines a large public sector infrastructure with a dynamic and rapidly growing private sector, catering to a population of over 1.4 billion people, nearly 65% of whom reside in rural areas. Delivering equitable, affordable, and quality healthcare at this scale is a formidable challenge.

The National Health Mission (NHM) has remained the backbone of India's public health system, strengthening rural and urban health services in the country. Under the Modi government, NHM investments have been scaled up, particularly in maternal and child health, infectious disease control, and non-communicable disease management. The Union Budget 2025–26 allocated **₹ 99,858.56 crore** to the Ministry of Health & Family Welfare, while broader expenditure on health-related programmes is projected to cross **₹ 1.35 lakh crore**, representing a nearly four-fold increase compared to **₹ 37,000 crore in 2013–14**.

This significant rise in investment is indicative of the government's policy shift toward recognizing healthcare as a central pillar of national progress.

1.2 Maternal and Child Health Improvements

India has recorded a remarkable decline in maternal and child health indicators over the past decade indicating appreciable improvement in health delivery efforts of the Government.

- **Maternal Mortality Ratio (MMR):** declined from **130 (2014–16) to 97** (2018–20), and further to **93 (2019–21)** per 100,000 live births.

- **Infant Mortality Rate (IMR):** reduced steadily with improved neonatal intensive care, universal immunization, and better maternal nutrition.
- **Total Fertility Rate (TFR):** The Total Fertility Rate (TFR) in India has reached replacement levels, marked a significant demographic milestone and placed the country among those with a stable population growth trajectory.

Interventions such as Janani Suraksha Yojana, Janani Shishu Suraksha Karyakram, and the Pradhan Mantri Surakshit Matritva Abhiyan, alongside improved rural outreach and also have been instrumental in achieving these gains.

1.3 Disease Control Achievements

Significant progress has been achieved in controlling communicable diseases:

- **Tuberculosis (TB):**

  Tuberculosis, historically known as a "disease of antiquity," remains a major public health challenge in terms of prevention, diagnosis, and management. Nevertheless, sustained and proactive governmental interventions have yielded measurable progress. Notably, the National TB Elimination Programme (NTEP) was launched by the Hon'ble Prime Minister of India, Shri Narendra Modi, as part of the government's commitment to ending TB in the country. The incidence of TB declined from **237 per 100,000 populations in 2015 to 195 per 100,000 in 2023**, representing a **17.7% reduction.**

  Innovative initiatives such as the **Nikshay Mitra programme**, enhanced private sector participation, and intensified active case-finding strategies have significantly contributed to reducing the burden of "missing cases." The continued consolidation of these measures is expected to accelerate progress towards the national goal of TB elimination.

- **Malaria:** Malaria has also sharp decline in morbidity and mortality, moving India closer to elimination targets.
- **Kala-azar:** Kala azar another infectious disease is also nearing elimination at the block level of the country.
- **Trachoma:** India has attained a landmark public health achievement with the official elimination of trachoma as a cause of blindness. This success reflects the sustained implementation of national blindness control programmes, adoption of WHO's SAFE strategy, and complementary initiatives in sanitation and hygiene.

Simultaneously, India's immunization landscape has been significantly strengthened through Mission Indradhanush and its intensified phases, which have moved the country closer to achieving near-universal vaccine coverage. These initiatives are further supported by digital innovations such as the U-WIN platform, a robust system for vaccine registration, tracking, and electronic certification, thereby ensuring greater efficiency, transparency, and accessibility in immunisation services.

1.4 Ayushman Bharat and Financial Protection

Ayushman Bharat, the financial protection insurance scheme popularly known as Ayushman Bharat Pradhan Mantri Jan Arogya Yojana (AB-PMJAY), is a flagship programme of the Modi Government. The **Ayushman Bharat initiative**, launched in 2018, stands as a landmark reform in India's health system. It has two critical pillars:

1. Pradhan Mantri Jan Arogya Yojana (PM-JAY):
    - Covers over **50 crore beneficiaries** with an annual health cover of **₹ 5 lakh per family**.

- More than **40 crore Ayushman cards have been issued.**
- A unique feature of this scheme is its portability, which ensures that migrant populations can access healthcare services across the nation. Additionally, Ayushman Bharat Health and Wellness Centres (HWCs) provide comprehensive primary healthcare under the same programme.
- Nearly 1.7 lakh centres operational, offering primary care, screening for non-communicable diseases, mental health support, and essential medicines.

By reducing out-of-pocket expenditure and widening access, PM-JAY has emerged as the **world's largest publicly funded health assurance scheme.**

1.5 Digital Health Transformation

The Digital India programme, a flagship initiative of the Modi government, represents another remarkable achievement, having fostered the development of a digital health ecosystem in the country and significantly reshaping access to healthcare for those in need.

The government's commitment to a digital health ecosystem has reshaped healthcare access:

- **Ayushman Bharat Digital Mission (ABDM):** Over **67 crore digital health IDs (ABHA)** generated, linking **42 crore health records** across verified hospitals and practitioners.
- **eSanjeevani Telemedicine Platform:** Delivered **tens of crores of consultations**, bridging rural–urban disparities.
- **Pradhan Mantri Bharatiya Janaushadhi Pariyojana (PMBJP)** is a unique government initiative that makes quality and affordable medicines, including generics,

accessible to patients through over 14,000 outlets across the country.

Together, these platforms are enabling India's transition toward a **paperless, citizen-centric digital health ecosystem.**

1.6 Women's Health and Innovation

Cervical cancer remains a major public health challenge in India, primarily caused by high-risk HPV infection. It accounts for over 100,000 new cases and nearly 60,000 deaths annually. Risk factors include early sexual activity, multiple partners, immunosuppression, and poor nutrition.

In 2024, India launched **Cervavac**, its first indigenously developed HPV vaccine, provided free to girls aged 9–14 and affordably priced for others. By preventing HPV infection before exposure, Cervavac is expected to avert thousands of cervical cancer cases annually.

Alongside vaccination, regular screening and health education are crucial for prevention. The launch of Cervavac reflects India's growing focus on **preventive, women-centric health innovations,** aiming to reduce the burden of cervical cancer and improve women's health outcomes.

2. Transformation in Medical Education

2.1 Historical Challenges and Our 2014 Publication

For decades, India's medical education faced multiple systemic barriers:

- Unequal distribution of colleges between urban and rural areas.
- Rapid, often unchecked privatization
- Non-transparent admission processes.
- Outdated curricula not aligned with global standards.

- Faculty shortages and limited faculty development opportunities.
- Weak research culture and inadequate incentives for innovation.

These issues were the subject of our earlier scholarly work. In **2014,** we published the article **"Medical Education in India: Current Challenges and Way Forward"** in *Medical Teacher (Early Online)*. This paper not only documented the structural deficiencies but also laid down a roadmap of potential reforms. It is significant to note that many of the changes implemented over the past decade resonate closely with the gaps and recommendations identified in that publication.

Thus, the trajectory of reforms in medical education can be seen as a **continuation of the academic discourse that we initiated in 2014** and now materialised through policy action of the present Government.

2.2 Expansion of Infrastructure and Seats

The growth in medical education capacity has been unprecedented:

- **Government medical colleges:** increased from **387** (2014) to **780** (2025).
- **MBBS seats:** more than doubled from **51,000** to **1.18 lakh.**
- **Postgraduate seats:** expanded from **31,000** to 74,000.

The establishment of new **AIIMS institutes** across the country as decentralised advanced training, of undergraduates and post graduates and super specialty and also bringing healthcare access to underserved regions.

2.3 Reforms in Admissions and Curriculum

- The introduction of the **National Eligibility-cum-Entrance Test (NEET)** as a single standardised entrance examination has ensured transparency and merit-based admissions across the country. Furthermore, the proposed National Exit Test (NEXT) is intended to serve as a single qualifying examination for undergraduate medical students and a basis for postgraduate admissions, representing a major shift in the medical education assessment system.

- **Competency-Based Medical Education (CBME):** Introduced in 2019, Competency-Based Medical Education (CBME) has brought a significant shift in the assessment of medical graduates. CBME emphasizes clinical skills, professional ethics, community health orientation, and critical reasoning, moving away from rote memorisation.
- **Faculty Development Programmes:** The recently established National Medical Commission (NMC) has introduced a new curriculum and overhauled medical regulation in India through comprehensive reforms. While the Faculty Development Programme (FDP) plays a crucial role in training skilled and competent faculty, there is a need to further strengthen it by establishing additional zonal and regional training centres. Upgrading the teaching capacity and assessment skills of existing training centres under the supervision of the NMC has already led to significant progress in this critical area.

To enhance faculty development further, it is proposed that state Health Universities, deemed universities, and other institutions offering undergraduate and postgraduate medical courses be designated as regional and zonal teacher training centres offering online / offline courses with the prior approval of NMC. This initiative would serve to bolster the Faculty Development

Programme and ensuring more robust and well-trained medical faculty across the country.

- **Research Promotion:** The Government of India has significantly bolstered its commitment to research and development (R&D) through substantial financial allocations. In the Union Budget for 2024–25, an ambitious ₹1 lakh crore corpus was announced under the Research, Development, and Innovation (RDI) scheme. This initiative aims to stimulate private sector investment in R&D, focusing on sunrise sectors such as artificial intelligence, quantum computing, and biotechnology. To kickstart this fund, the Department of Science and Technology (DST) has been allocated ₹20,000 crore in the 2025–26 budget. Additionally, the establishment of the Anusandhan National Research Foundation (ANRF) through the ANRF Act of 2023 provides strategic direction for research, innovation, and entrepreneurship across various domains, including health, agriculture, and technology. These initiatives underscore the government's dedication to fostering a robust research ecosystem and driving innovation across the country.

These reforms are steering India away from a purely quantity-driven approach toward a more balanced **quantity–quality paradigm.**

3. Global Context and Emerging Opportunities

India's reforms have placed it firmly on the path toward **Universal Health Coverage (UHC)**, aligning with the **UN Sustainable Development Goals (SDG-3)**. Simultaneously, medical education reforms are making India a potential hub for **global health workforce training.**

Medical tourism, projected to grow rapidly, benefits from India's **unique blend of affordability, quality, and advanced**

infrastructure. This sector alone is estimated to contribute billions to the economy annually.

4. Challenges and the Way Forward

Despite impressive gains, challenges remain:

1. **Healthcare Delivery Gaps**
    - Rural–urban disparities in health infrastructure and specialist availability.
    - Persistent high out-of-pocket expenditure despite PM-JAY coverage.
2. **Medical Education Quality Concerns**
    - Shortage of qualified faculty in many new colleges.
    - Need for stronger accreditation and quality monitoring.
    - Limited integration of research with clinical practice.
3. **Emerging Health Priorities**
    - Rising burden of non-communicable diseases (diabetes, hypertension, cancer).
    - Mental health crisis, particularly among youth and medical professionals.
    - Antimicrobial resistance and new infectious disease threats.
4. **Systemic Reforms Required**
    - Greater investment in primary healthcare.
    - Expansion of digital health literacy among citizens.
    - Strengthening of public health research institutions.
    - Focus on climate change and environmental health challenges.

5. Conclusion

In the past eleven years, India has witnessed a **paradigm shift in healthcare and medical education**. By expanding infrastructure, building digital platforms, ensuring financial protection, and reforming medical curricula, the country has moved closer to achieving universal health coverage.

The form the challenges we documented in **our 2014 article on medical education** to the achievements of 2025 illustrates not only policy responsiveness but also the resilience and adaptability of India's systems. Looking ahead, the focus must shift from quantity to quality, from access to excellence, and from treatment to prevention. If sustained, these reforms have the potential to make India not just a **global leader in healthcare delivery and medical education**, but also a **model of inclusive, innovative, and sustainable health systems** for the 21st century.

References

1. Business Standard. (2024, November 2). India records 17.7% decline in TB incidence from 2015 to 2023: WHO report. Retrieved from https://www.business-standard.com/health/india-records-17-7-decline-in-tb-incidence-from-2015-to-2023-who-report-124110200792_1.html
2. Fortune India. (2023, March 17). India's Maternal Mortality Ratio declines to 97 per lakh in 2018–2020. Retrieved from https://www.fortuneindia.com/macro/indias-maternal-mortality-ratio-declines-to-97-per-lakh-in-2018-2020/110570
3. Ministry of Health & Family Welfare. (2023). Press Information Bureau Release: TB incidence and mortality trends. Government of India. Retrieved from https://www.pib.gov.in/PressReleasePage.aspx?PRID=2070942
4. Ministry of Health & Family Welfare. (2024). Ayushman Bharat Digital Mission progress report. Government of India. Retrieved from https://www.pib.gov.in/PressReleasePage.aspx?PRID=2059537
5. The Times of India. (2025a, January 27). Union Budget 2025 health highlights and announcements. Retrieved from https://timesofindia.indiatimes.com/life-style/health-fitness/health-news/union-budget-2025-health-highlights-and-announcements/articleshow/117816332.cms

6. The Times of India. (2025b, February 20). Marked improvement in maternal, child health indicators: Government. Retrieved from https://timesofindia.indiatimes.com/india/marked-improvement-in-maternal-child-health-indicators-government/articleshow/121066578.cms
7. The Times of India. (2025, March 5). Amit Shah slams Congress over poor health budget since Independence, showcases BJP's feat since 2014. Retrieved from https://timesofindia.indiatimes.com/city/nagpur/amit-shah-slams-cong-over-poor-health-budget-since-independence-showcases-bjps-health-feat-since-2014/articleshow/121421361.cms
8. The Knowledge Academy. (2025). How many MBBS seats are there in NEET 2025? Retrieved from https://www.theknowledgeacademy.com/blog/how-many-seats-are-there-in-neet/
9. Ensure Education. (2025). NEET 2025 cut-off for government MBBS colleges: State-wise category-wise with total seats in India. Retrieved from https://www.ensureeducation.com/blog/neet-2025-cut-off-for-government-mbbs-colleges-state-wise-category-wise-with-total-seats-in-india
10. Solanki, A., & Kashyap, S. (2014). Medical education in India: Current challenges and way forward. Medical Teacher (Early Online), 1–5.
11. Government of India. (2024). *Union Budget 2024–25: Research, Develop-ment and Innovation (RDI) scheme.* Press Information Bureau. Retrieved from https://www.pib.gov.in/PressReleasePage.aspx?PRID=2141130
12. Government of India. (2025). *Department of Science and Technology: Budget allocation for 2025–26.* Press Information Bureau. Retrieved from https://www.pib.gov.in
13. PRS India. (2023). *The Anusandhan National Research Foundation Bill, 2023.* Retrieved from https://prsindia.org/billtrack/the-anusandhan-national-research-foundation-bill-2023

37

Prime Minister Shri Narendra Modi: A Visionary Leader Transforming India through his Observation and Analytical Power

Dr. Tankeshwar Kumar[1]

Prime Minister Narendra Modi stands as a leader with exceptional observational power and analytical power. With nearly six decades of experience in public life, he has shown a unique ability to understand developments at the grassroots level, analyze societal needs, and translate those observations into impactful policies. His leadership is marked by foresight—planning not just for the next five years, but for the many decades to come, laying the groundwork for India's emergence as a global powerhouse.

During the past 11 years of his prime ministership, Prime Minister Modi has addressed core challenges facing the Indian population. From launching the Swachh Bharat Abhiyan to improve sanitation and public health, to Startup India and Skill India to foster innovation and employability, and from building world-class infrastructure to launching Ayushman Bharat for universal healthcare, his government has worked to

1. Vice-Chancellor, Central University of Haryana, Mahendergarh

elevate millions from poverty line and create an India of dignity and opportunity. One of the most impactful areas of reform, however, has been education, where a new vision for the future has been articulated and systematically implemented.

The launch of the National Education Policy (NEP) 2020 was a turning point in India's education history. Unlike earlier policies that focused primarily on access and literacy, NEP 2020 is a comprehensive, inclusive, and future-ready framework. It emphasizes flexibility, multidisciplinarity, and practical learning, moving away from rigid subject boundaries and rote-based instruction and learning. Students are now empowered to pursue combinations of subjects based on their interests and career aspirations, making education more learner-centric.

Among the key features of NEP is the Multiple Entry and Exit (ME-ME) system, which allows students to exit and re-enter academic programmes with appropriate certification—providing continuity without academic loss. This is supported by the Academic Bank of Credits (ABC), which enables students to accumulate and transfer credits across institutions and disciplines. These innovations provide the much-needed flexibility and resilience for a diverse and dynamic student population.

NEP also places a strong emphasis on vocational education and skill development, with a target of ensuring that 50% of learners have exposure to vocational training by 2025. This will bridge the long-standing gap between academic learning and industry expectations. Furthermore, the promotion of education in regional and mother tongues during the foundational years is set to make learning more inclusive and effective, especially for students from rural and marginalised backgrounds.

Perhaps the most forward-looking aspect of NEP is its focus on integrating research and innovation into the mainstream academic structure, which has been further institutionalised through the creation of the Anusandhan National Research Foundation (ANRF). With a proposed funding of many thousands crore over five years, ANRF is envisioned as a central agency to promote high-quality research, encourage collaboration between academia and industry, and support young innovators and institutions across disciplines. It aims to build a research ecosystem that is not only globally competitive but also nationally relevant, focusing on areas like healthcare, agriculture, clean energy, digital technologies, and defence.

The ANRF will act as a catalyst in transforming Indian universities from teaching-centric institutions into research-intensive hubs, driving innovation and economic development. By connecting academic institutions with industry, ANRF ensures that research outcomes contribute to real-world applications and national priorities.

Together, NEP 2020 and ANRF reflect the Modi government's commitment to building an education system for the 21st century—one that empowers every student, supports every teacher, and aligns India's academic ambitions with global standards. These reforms are not just about changing the structure of education—they are about reshaping the destiny of the nation.

In conclusion, Prime Minister Narendra Modi's leadership in the field of education shows a deep understanding of India's challenges and immense confidence in its youth. By focusing on flexibility, employability, innovation, and research, he is preparing the nation not just for the present, but for the next fifty years and beyond. Through visionary reforms like NEP and ANRF, he is creating an education system that is inclusive, future-ready, and globally respected—a true cornerstone of India's rise as a knowledge superpower before 2047.

Index